Gardens through time

Gardens
through time

JANE OWEN & DIARMUID GAVIN

'For Gaie and Toby,
who gave me Eden'

Jane Owen

This book is published
to accompany the
BBC Television series
Gardens Through Time
Executive producers:
*Jill Lourie and Charles
Wace*
Series producer:
Hannah Wyatt
Commissioning Executive
for the BBC: *Celia Taylor*

Published by BBC Books,
BBC Worldwide Ltd
Woodlands
80 Wood Lane
London W12 0TT

First published 2004
Text © copyright
Jane Owen
except Chapter 8
© copyright
Diarmuid Gavin
The moral right of the
authors has been asserted.

ISBN 0 563 48715 1

Commissioning Editor:
Vivien Bowler
Project Editor:
Helena Caldon
Copy Editor:
Steve Dobell
Cover Art Director:
Pene Parker
Book Designer:
Andrew Barron
Picture Researcher:
Rachel Jordan
Garden plans:
Nancy Nicholson
Production Controller:
Christopher Tinker

Set in Quay Sans and
Proforma

Printed and bound in Italy
by LEGO SpA
Colour separations by
Butler & Tanner Ltd,
England

For more information about
this and other BBC books,
please visit our website on
www.bbcshop.com

Contents

Introduction

Opposite: A window on the world as laid out in a few Staffordshire acres at Biddulph Grange. This area is 'China'.

There's a joke going round the gardening world at the moment. One garden expert asks another to describe a hyped new garden: 'Oh, you know – same plants, different order,' comes the reply. How very different it was two hundred years ago, when this story begins. Then plants were big news, whatever order they were put in. Many were new to this country and they caused a sensation – so much so that they were one of the driving forces behind a new garden style. In fact the new plants were part of the revolution that created our first suburban gardens, the type most of us have today. This book, which is part of the Royal Horticultural Society's two hundredth anniversary celebrations, tells the story of those gardens – our own backyards which, however recently they were made, owe so much to the last two centuries.

Today we live in the age of the instant make-over, in which people, houses, rooms and now gardens can be transformed with a couple of well-filled T-shirts and a wheelbarrow. For most of us, though, any change in our gardens is gradual, the result of hard work and hard cash – often applied in fits and starts, and somehow never quite finished.

My grandfather's Nottinghamshire garden was typical. In less than an acre there was a nineteenth-century-style Italianate area, an early twentieth-century rose pergola, overgrown yews and dripping limes planted in the Victorian age, a pond swarming with tiny frogs (very today), and a vegetable plot that began life when Britain was digging for victory during the Second World War. To my childish eye this hotchpotch of designs was pure magic; from an historian's point of view, it was a living document – an accumulation of fashions, the garden equivalent of geological strata.

If some established gardens and parks tell several stories, others tell one alone. They are sleeping beauties that rest on their laurels (literally in some cases) without accumulating any design bar their first. This struck me when I worked, briefly, in the flower garden at London's Waterlow Park during my gap year

in the 1970s. The techniques that I was taught, and the colourful displays of massed bedding that I nurtured, were in a time warp going back to the mid nineteenth century; and the annual routine of taking cuttings guaranteed the same selection of flowers, and similar designs, year after year.

I was fond of the dazzling bedding schemes, less so the rule that women had to take tea breaks in their own bothy rather than being allowed a little R&R with the men – a disappointment after years at a girls' boarding school. This gender separation probably dated back to the early twentieth century, when women gardeners were first employed in public gardens amid a torrent of misogynist press comment.

The story to be told in this book begins two centuries ago, in 1804, when the Horticultural Society began life (it took a few decades to become Royal). For the sake of convenience, I've sliced up the 200-year period since then into seven chapters, each focused on a particular garden style. These snapshots have been brought to life at the Royal Horticultural Society's Harlow Carr garden, in Yorkshire, where we have created seven display gardens for the *Gardens Through Time* television series. I strongly recommend you to go and see them.

The gardens, this book and the series are complementary, and what appears in one won't necessarily appear in the other. The gardens intentionally ignore evolutionary design in order to give seven uncluttered pictures of fashionable middle-class gardens. In this book I have no such constraints, so I've been able to explore cutting-edge gardens where vogues began, as well as the controversy and argument that helped to shape them.

For instance, at the start of the nineteenth century Nature was all the rage, and so were native plants (just as they are today). Within a few decades Nature was booted out of the garden to make way for exotic plant material from all over the world. This glimpse of garden history conveys one of the themes of this book: gardeners have always veered between formal and less formal, invasive and less invasive ways in which to garden. A century before our story begins, the theme is aired by the poet Alexander Pope, one of the founders of the English Landscape Movement, that great reaction against seventeenth-century formality. In 1719 he describes a heated meeting between fashionable gardeners and the future George II's wife, Caroline, who was making a garden at Richmond Lodge, now part of Kew:

One declar'd he would not have too much Art in it, for [his] notion of gardening is, that it is only sweeping Nature … There were some who could not bear Ever-greens, and called them Never-greens; some, who were angry at them only when they were cut into shapes, and gave the modern Gard'ners the name of Ever-greens Taylors; some who had no dislike to Cones and Cubes, but wou'd have 'em cut in Forest-trees; and some who were in a passion against any thing in shape, even against clipt hedges, which they call'd green walls.

Queen Caroline died in 1737 owing £20,000, an awesome amount by present-day standards. A lot of her money was lavished on land-scaping part of Kew Gardens. The funny thing is that some of the structures installed at eighteenth-century Kew were pretty flimsy – made from wood coated with stone-effect plaster finish. It was even said that the Palladian Bridge and Temple of Victory were built in a night. So the next time we are tempted to sneer at 'instant' gardens on television, perhaps we should think back to eighteenth-century Kew.

History repeats itself, and even garden features have an uncanny way of doing the historical rounds. Whenever you've a moment between weeding, barrowing, pruning, sowing, reaping and armchair gardening, try playing 'spot the genuinely innovative feature'. There aren't many. A wall-mounted water feature is a miniature echo of those at the Villa d'Este's sixteenth-century water gardens in Italy. Piped music can be compared to the hydraulic-powered birdsong of seventeenth-century gardens. The current craze for vibrant, clashing plant colour has its Victorian equivalents. Even decks are no more than terraces – which can be traced back to Babylon.

Garden makers from every generation reinvent traditional features and weave their personalities into gardens as they create and maintain them. And, heaven knows, we're a mixed bunch – because garden-making winds its irresistible tendrils around anyone, whatever their class, race, creed or inside leg measurement. It makes most of us very happy and, by the by, makes millionaires of some and bankrupts of others. Queen Caroline's financial advisers must have cursed gardening – and those advising the Edwardian heiress and plantswoman Ellen Willmott can't have been much happier. Miss Willmott, who, incidentally, sometimes carried a gun in her handbag, spent her fortune on her garden at Warley Place in Essex, which she ran with the help of legions of liveried gardeners. She died in penury in 1934. I can think of several contemporary

designers and plant collectors who also live impoverished lives for the love of gardens. Settling that against the millions of pounds raised for charity by the National Gardens Scheme highlights one of many contradictions in the seductive world of gardens.

Seductive it most certainly is. I can't be the only one who spends wakeful nights reshaping the landscape, moving trees, transforming colour schemes and wondering whether Catherine the Great really did scatter diamonds across her garden to add a little night-time twinkle. There are none in my garden, sadly, but I know I am not the only one who weeds and hunts slugs by torchlight after a day at the office. Obsessive? You bet. It's a British obsession that can be seen from space. Satellite pictures show an intricate pattern of parks and gardens softening the black and grey of our urban areas. More than one third of London alone is green, and there are networks of gardens stretching through cities, towns, suburbs and villages the length and breadth of the country. The British love making gardens – and we're rather good at it. It is our defining passion and one that makes me neglect to sleep at this euphoric, bud-popping time of year.

Jane Owen
Shill House, Summer 2004

1 Plant Power, Plant Passion
A Garden Revolution in the Early Nineteenth Century

Opposite: Eschscholtzia californica, *the Californian poppy, was introduced to Britain in 1825. The flower is pictured here with* Cerinthe major *'Purpurascens',* Nigella damascena *and* Atriplex hortensis *var.* rubra.

Mr Hatchard's bookshop-cum-coffee-shop on Piccadilly, an early nineteenth-century version of Starbucks, was a well-established venue for meeting, gossiping and plotting. This was where anti-slave trade papers would one day be discussed. On 7 March 1804 seven men met there with a less politically sensitive agenda – they wanted to start a Horticultural Society, the first of its kind. This momentous meeting is recorded in a heavy volume bound in red leather and now stored in the Society's internet-friendly, atmosphere-controlled library – quite a contrast to Mr Hatchard's smoky rooms where the Society began life.

1768–71
Sir Joseph Banks sails on Captain Cook's HMS *Endeavour*. He returns with *Gaultheria mucronata*, *Phormium tenax*, *Banksia integrifolia* and much more

1783
American War of Independence ends

1789
French Revolution begins

1798
Wordsworth publishes *Lyrical Ballads* and introduces Romanticism to English poetry

1801
Royal Garden at Kew is joined with the garden at Kew House to make the Royal Botanic Gardens

1804
Horticultural Society founded
Dahlia coccinea, Turk's cap and tiger lily introduced

1805
Battle of Trafalgar

1811
Prince of Wales becomes Prince Regent
Humphry Repton visits Endsleigh

1814
Steam-driven printing press invented

1815
Napoleonic Wars end – and the Continent reopens to tourism
Jane Austen publishes *Persuasion*

1816
Bleeding heart and *Wisteria sinensis* introduced

1820
Prince Regent comes to the throne as George IV

1821
Horticultural Society gardens open at Chiswick

1822
John Loudon's *Encyclopaedia of Gardening* published
Calceolaria corymbosa introduced
1823
David Douglas plant hunts in America for the Horticultural Society

1824
Child prodigy Franz Listz's piano playing takes Paris by storm
1825
California poppy introduced
First scheduled passenger train service begins, in Darlington
1826
Loudon's the *Gardener's Magazine* launched.
Ribes sanguineum introduced by David Douglas
1828
Garrya elliptica introduced
1830
Lawnmower invented
1831
Darwin sails with HMS *Beagle*
1835
The Terrace Garden opens in Gravesend, the first purpose-built public park
1838
The Suburban Gardener and Villa Companion published

Below: The Horticultural Society's garden at Chiswick, where plants were trialled and displayed from 1821. This is where the Duke of Devonshire talent-spotted Joseph Paxton.

Then the Horticultural Society had no garden, let alone a library. It simply had a mission:

'To form a repository for all the knowledge which can be collected on...[horticulture], and to give a stimulus to the exertions of individuals for its further improvement.' Within twenty years it had leased a garden at Chiswick for plant trials, challenged Kew's supremacy, and increased the number of its fellows (members) from seven to 1,500. The Horticultural Society had identified and filled a gaping hole in the market: it created a focus for the plant craze that was to reinvent the garden.

The plant craze went beyond fashionable flowers. Plants were money-spinners, and they were crucial to the British Empire. Without cotton, chocolate, sugar, rubber and coffee, and the trade they stimulated, the British economy would have been a shadow of itself. Without the quinine-rich cinchona tree, fewer colonialists would have survived malaria-infested Africa, India or the Far East. Plants were hot property, so much so that, at the Royal Botanic Gardens, Kew, visitors had to be policed, one to one, by gardeners. One nursery manager who apparently evaded his minders was tried for the crime of plant theft at the Old Bailey. He was accused of taking introductions or 'new' plants, which could be

sold for a fortune to fashionable gardeners and botanists. He was let off on a technicality.

Unlike Kew, which specialized in part in the research and development of economically useful crops, the Horticultural Society was interested in ornamental and productive plants that could be used in domestic gardens. It was also interested in pooling the skills and knowledge of nurserymen, head gardeners and enthusiastic amateurs who were faced with increasing numbers of 'new' plants.

The New Gardens
There was plenty of skill and knowledge to pool. The British had a reputation for cultivating some of the finest plants available – and while the Napoleonic Wars raged, style-conscious Empress Josephine of France bought her rose plants from a British grower.

This horticultural expertise and passion for plants transformed the scale, design and

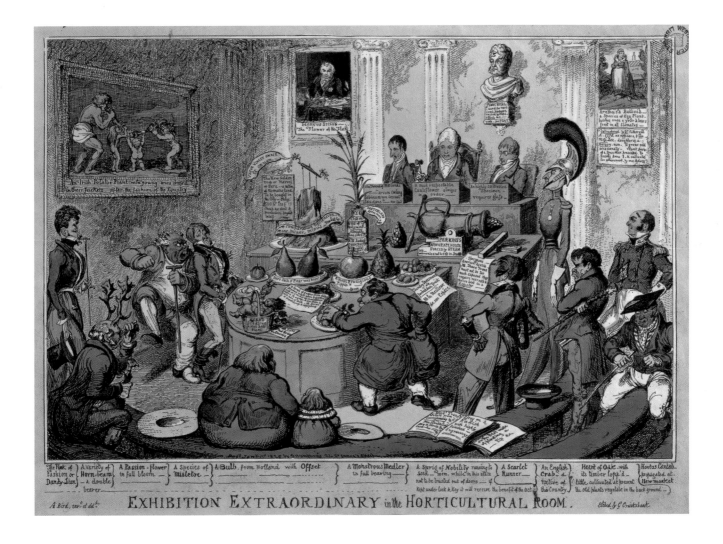

EXHIBITION EXTRAORDINARY in the HORTICULTURAL ROOM.

structure of fashionable British gardens. It was also well timed because the new middle class, the people coming into money through the Industrial Revolution, needed a new type of garden to complement the smart villas they were building around towns and cities. They were a substantial force – around 1,700,000 in 1815 – and they became increasingly powerful during the century. The new garden owners wanted a lot more than an old-fashioned, sooty city plot where jobbing gardeners installed trellis for privacy along with a few seasonal flowers. Their gardens needed to reflect their elevated social status as well as the prevailing Romantic mood. On the other hand, their gardens rarely measured more than a few acres and were therefore too small

for the landscapes made fashionable by eighteenth-century landowners. Then Nature (with a little help from man) ruled supreme, and dictated an outward-looking style using views of distant fields and woodlands as part of the overall effect. Villa owners who tried building miniature versions of these grand schemes were lampooned mercilessly.

All the same, fashionable landscapers, such as Humphry Repton, were commissioned to design middle-class gardens, as Repton himself records in 1816: '...villas, are daily springing up; and these, with a few acres...have, of late, had the greatest claim on my attention'.

Repton helped to set the scene for smaller-scale garden design, but it was the great designer,

Above: The newly formed Horticultural Society was the talk of London and attracted Cruikshank's satirical attention in January 1826. On the left of the cartoon a raging gent with a walking stick becomes a 'passion flower in full bloom'. On the right the book open at an 'Essay on a Radish' would have had a ring of truth for the early meetings – they tended to focus on fruit and vegetables rather than ornamental plants.

writer, editor and campaigner John Loudon
who popularized a coherent new villa garden
style. Villa owners who could not afford to
employ someone as smart as Repton could
copy designs published in Loudon's journal,
the *Gardener's Magazine*, after its launch in
1826. The designs were inward-looking and
focused on specimen trees, flowers and shrubs
rather than distant views. Layouts were
informal and irregular, with curving gravel or
clinker paths circulating around a lawn
planted with groups of trees or beds of mixed
flowers. Chic gardens had to include new
plants, which were often displayed in pots, as
we shall see. Common flowers were displayed
in what we would now call island beds, more

usually associated with 1970s' suburbia.

These were a feature of an influential flower
garden made by William Mason and Earl
Harcourt in the 1770s at Nuneham Courtenay
in Oxfordshire. Serpentine paths led around
a lawn dotted with rare trees and irregular-
shaped, box-edged beds bursting with shrubs
and plants such as hollyhocks. Typically for
the eighteenth century, the flower garden was
hidden from the house and landscape by trees
so that it did not disturb the 'natural' landscape
scenery – created, in Nuneham Courtenay's
case, by moving an entire village to improve
the view. Audley End in Suffolk included
another example of a concealed flower garden.

Tall trees hid beds of colourful, height-coordinated flowers set into a lawn. This style, and the island beds in particular, were ideal for the relatively small gardens around villas.

Island beds could be transformed into 'flower baskets' with edgings of looped iron or wicker to give the effect of a giant basket of flowers. Some even had a wicker or wire 'handle' arching over the centre of the bed to complete the picture, and some were painted green. The great thing about flower baskets was that they were fashionable enough to be installed by one of the richest families in the country, the Rothschilds, and yet they were modest enough, in size and cost, to fit into villa gardens. The Rothschilds installed flower baskets at their country estate, Gunnersbury, now a West London park, where flower baskets can still be seen. These ingenious features may have been invented by Repton, who used them to help landowners integrate flower gardens with surrounding landscapes. At Sheringham Hall in Norfolk, for instance, Repton suggested that flower baskets dot the lawn in front of the house, which was fenced from the surrounding hills and woodland by low trellis. He used a similar trellis effect in 1814 at Endsleigh in Devon, where a wide lawn terrace made the transition between Repton's formal flowery terraces, rather than

flower baskets, and the magnificent woods and hills of the Tamar valley.

The irregular, informal style of early nineteenth-century flower gardens was gradually overtaken. John Loudon, whose *Gardener's Magazine* and books were as much a source as a symptom of new garden styles, began by recommending irregular design. All that changed after he, like many of his contemporaries, made a tour of the post-war Continent. Loudon arrived back brimming with new ideas about the need for regular, symmetrical shapes in the new century's flower gardens. This formal, symmetrical layout would dominate mid nineteenth-century garden style.

Features and Ornaments

The new flower garden was arranged around the villa rather than being concealed. Beyond it were usually several different areas. While the kitchen garden was often walled and therefore out of sight, less formal ornamental areas, such as woodland walks, were designed to be seen from the flower garden. Walks could be punctuated by seats, some of them covered, where people could sit and admire the view, or talk in privacy away from prying ears of parents or chaperones. Jane Austen's Wood Walk at Steventon

GENERAL VIEW FROM THE SOUTH AND EAST FRONTS OF THE

Rectory in Hampshire, for instance, had the occasional bench.

Wood Walk was probably a kind of shrubbery, an important feature in any contemporary garden, as the historian Mavis Batey makes clear in her meticulous and engaging work on Regency gardens. Most were evergreen structures, jazzed up by roses, pinks,

columbines, lilacs, sweet Williams and jasmine. Today's shrubberies rarely look as they would have in Regency times because they have grown too high and lost the plants that once gave them colour, scent and interest.

Robust plants were used in the shrubbery, while expensive and tender ones were sometimes considered too precious to be

COTTAGE AT ENDSLEIGH, DEVONSHIRE. — DUTCHESS OF BEDFORD

planted out at all, even in the main flower
garden. Instead these were kept in pots, which
could be taken inside at the first hint of frost.
Pot plants were important enough to be
itemized in Princess Augusta's will. The
Princess, George III's mother, who landscaped
much of Kew, died in 1772 and left '320 pots of
stocks, verbena etc, 60 pots of geraniums, one
large myrtle and two large white azaleas in

tubs and 18 cacti; 170 ericas; 350 geraniums on
platforms'. The platforms were probably plant
stands, tiered or otherwise. These could be
simple wooden affairs or far more elaborate
structures with tiles set into a metal frame
mounted on castors so that they could move
around the house and/or garden. Specialized
plant stands, auricula theatres, were essentially
a series of shelves, with a roof to protect the

auricula's delicate 'paste' or floury centre from rain. Sometimes the theatres were painted black – to show off the flowers – and often they were built with mirrors at either side.

Garden ornamentation went beyond pots and flower stands. Arches, constructed from metal or rustic wood, supported climbers, especially scented climbers such as jasmine, honeysuckle and roses. Rustic ornaments were ubiquitous, mostly knocked up on the spot by the gardeners. This was not a money-saving device – this was Fashion. At the turn of the century Queen Charlotte, George III's wife, had a pair of 'Bath rustick chairs composed of horticultural implements and cane seated'; a thatched rustic tea-house made from various different woods, all 'with the bark still on' – and a hammock, 'made from the bark of the cocoa tree, of very ingenious workmanship'. Ingenious, no doubt, but uncomfortable by the sound of it. Rustic benches were also common, and so were barrow benches,

FIG. 48.—MOVEABLE GARDEN SEAT.

which had wheels at one end and barrow-like handles at the other for easy movement around the garden. For occasions such as tea parties and other such outdoor events, servants would carry out chairs and tables from the house or 'cottage' to add to existing garden furniture.

Gardens were entertaining places, in every sense of the word, and excellent venues for romance, as Jane Austen records in *Mansfield Park* (1814): 'A young woman, pretty, lively, with a harp as elegant as herself; and both placed near a window, cut to the ground, and opening onto a little lawn, surrounded by shrubs in the rich foliage of summer, was enough to catch any man's heart.'

The Picturesque

Austen satirized contemporary garden vogues but she, like the German novelist, scientist and poet Johann Goethe, described scenes which would have been considered fashionably 'picturesque' by contemporaries. The label was used a great deal at the turn of the eighteenth and nineteenth centuries, and it could mean anything from a wild, rocky, bandit-infested landscape to an intimate rural scene conjured up by woodland and a rustic bridge. Broadly, picturesque could mean a landscape inspired by pictures, or a landscape

Opposite: Scotney Castle is a superb example of Regency picturesque, with views of the ruins framed by trees.

that inspired pictures. Picturesque landscape was especially fashionable when Continental travel was stopped by the Napoleonic Wars, and domestic scenery became the focus of artistic and tourist attention.

One type of picturesque was expressed to perfection at 1830s' Scotney Castle in Kent. A ruined, moated castle stood above a derelict quarry. This dramatic scene was framed by groups of trees planted at strategic points around the estate. Picturesque landscapes depended on drama or even danger – for example, a precipitous path along a cliff top – rather than the smooth and ordered landscapes made by eighteenth-century landscapers such as Capability Brown. These new landscapes were fashionably romantic – a *frisson* of danger in a beautiful landscape gave an ideal setting for liaisons, dangerous or otherwise. In villa gardens picturesque features could include magnificent trees or a type of shrubbery, made up of native or woodland plants, that gave the impression of the outer fringes of a natural wilderness. Austen made a version at Chawton Cottage with a structure of thorns, broom and evergreen cheered up by lilac.

The garden at the Prince Regent's Royal Cottage (later Royal Lodge) was described,

Below: The picnic room of Queen Charlotte's cottage at Kew was probably painted by Princess Elizabeth. Such paintings and botanizing were favoured by royalty, aristocracy and, increasingly, the middle classes.

in 1828, as 'picturesque'. His flowery garden was certainly the antithesis of stately eighteenth-century parkland. Just down the road from Royal Cottage his father, George III, had begun to give Windsor Castle a picturesque makeover, but the Prince Regent had, voguishly, turned his back on palace life and gone for the 'simple' alternative. He had Royal Cottage radically redesigned by John Nash with a 'rustic columned Viranda [sic]...covered with a thatched roof and paved with hexagonal Tiles'. Honeysuckle and other flowering creepers tumbled over the veranda around the 'cottage'; rustic fences marked the boundaries, and planting was organized to obscure any sign of habitation. Pictures published around this time show 'His majesty's cottage' surrounded by colourful borders, and a contemporary caricature of the royals 'rusticating' at Royal Cottage shows them digging, watering the garden with a pump and hose, and pushing a wheelbarrow – *plus ça change...*

The Prince Regent and his friends epitomized all the latest trends. They embraced the cosy intimacy of the early nineteenth century and moved from their palaces and grand piles into 'cottages' (spacious houses by twenty-first-century standards) where they could enjoy botanizing and gardening.

One of the Prince Regent's sisters, Princess Elizabeth, made up for the fact that she was still stuck in a palace by decorating the picnic room of a fashionable rustic cottage at Kew with nasturtiums and convolvulus twined around Gothic arches of bamboo. Her family connections ensured that she was up to date with gardening style.

The Gardening Press

Gardeners down the social scale kept up with the latest trends via the newly created gardening press. John Loudon launched the *Gardener's Magazine* in 1826, about a decade after the monthly illustrated *Botanical Cabinet* and forty years after what is probably the first gardening journal, the *Botanical Magazine.* The latter included exquisite, hand-coloured engravings of plant introductions. More than half a dozen magazines followed, including Joseph Paxton's *Magazine of Botany and Gardening* and the *Horticultural Register.*

Magazines and books described gardens as well as plants. Loudon's extensive and well-publicized write-ups of garden tours gave vivid, if rather opinionated, descriptions. Some preferred to see gardens for themselves; garden visiting was already a favoured pastime. The system was straightforward: 'carriage folk' were welcome. They were

Below: Calceolarias first arrived from South America in the late eighteenth century. By the mid nineteenth century they were bedding stars.

obviously people of substance. Others were not admitted – until the advent of the railways, which brought punters right into, or within walking distance of, estates such as Alton Towers and Mount Edgcumbe. Unlike carriage folk, who would turn up individually with little or no warning, the railway visitors would be admitted on certain specified days, when they were charged an entrance fee (often high – around a shilling) and monitored during their visit.

So, inspired by the gardening press and by garden visits, the middle classes became the new patrons of garden making, or, as Loudon puts it in one of his garden tours: 'Almost the only highly kept gardens which we saw were those of small proprietors, professional men, merchants or bankers.'

The Latest Floral Fashions

Fashionable plots had to include 'new' plants, such as ivy-leaved geraniums, variegated geraniums, *Salvia splendens* and *Calceolaria corymbosa*, to name but a few. These came to Britain in a variety of ways. Plant hunters' accounts sometimes give the impression that every introduced plant involved death-defying adventures in some dangerously foreign and therefore uncivilized land. In fact, nurseries in China and America were the source of some plants, while others were collected by traders and sea captains going about their normal business. Dr John Duncan, an East India Company officer, introduced the tree peony in 1787, although seven years later it had to be replaced with plants sent by Daniel and Thomas Beale, brothers who traded in China and India. By this time there was also a fledgling international plant trade. For instance, John Bartram and his son, William, introduced many new plants to Britain from their native Pennsylvania – in 1773 they sent over *Hydrangea quercifolia*, the oak-leaved variety.

All the same, many professional plant hunters, particularly in the early nineteenth century, did take considerable risks to collect plants, and many died on the job. In 1823 the Horticultural Society commissioned their first plant hunter, David Douglas of the eponymous fir, to go to North America. Douglas died eleven years later in Hawaii after falling into a pit trap with a wild bull. His introductions included *Garrya elliptica*, godetias, the poached egg plant, the flowering currant and a mass of pines, including Sitka spruce.

It was a while before nurseries could offer their customers introductions in any number. The high cost of those that were available, coupled with the plants' precarious grip on life, dictated a Spartan planting style. Specimens were arranged singly, with plenty of bare earth around them.

The problem was that new arrivals, from *Phormium tenax* to the tiger lily, were mysteries in terms of their cultivation, so survival rates were unpredictable. The early nineteenth-century painting *Golding Constable's Flower Garden* (John Constable's picture of his mother's flower garden painted in 1815 – see pages 30–1) shows a typically simple layout.

New introductions inspired what would now be called plantsmen's gardens...and they were not always a success, as Maria Elizabeth Jackson describes in her 1812 book *The Florist's Manual* (subtitled *Hints for the Construction of a Gay Flower-Garden*):

Fashionable novices are seduced by nursery catalogues into parting with huge sums of money for rare new plants (many simply common plants with a new name) or genuinely new introductions. They paint plant names on numerous labels which are pushed beside the newly installed specimen and then wait for the coming to season only to face humiliation. The novice's garden is a sea of labels, whereas her neighbour's less fashionable plot is a 'brilliant glow'.

The brilliant glow probably came from so-called florists' flowers, which were well tried and readily available. The distinction was important to contemporaries, and in 1829 William Cobbett, who had a shop in Fleet Street and wrote *The English Gardener*, explained that florists' flowers were put into unfashionable 'beds' whereas 'borders' were planted with a range of colour- and height-coordinated plants to give year-round interest.

A Gardener's Life

Maria Elizabeth Jackson was one of those who elevated the benefits of gardening to almost mystical status. She prescribed gardening as an aid to women's mental and physical well-being. By the mid century, Loudon's devoted wife Jane, an author in her own right, suggested gardening as an activity morally superior to bowls or shooting. People's attitudes to gardening had shifted radically since the eighteenth century, and this is illustrated by the updating of *Every Man His Own Gardener* by Thomas Mawe and John Abercrombie. When the book was first published, in the 1770s, the frontispiece showed a gardener at work. The 1804 edition showed an almost identical scene but, instead of a gardener, a well-dressed gentleman is wielding the spade.

Gradually, gardening, as opposed to botanizing or making a herbarium, came to be seen as a gentlemanly and even ladylike occupation. While some enthusiasts designed their gardens and did a little gentlemanly or ladylike pottering, the donkey work would still have been left to local garden contractors or head gardeners. Despite their importance, information about gardeners' working lives is patchy. Large estates usually recorded gardeners' pay and conditions, but the same is not true of the gardeners who worked in and around towns. Some head gardeners had their own staff cottages, a good salary and, sometimes, an opportunity to travel the world and to expound their theories in the horticultural press. Journeyman gardeners, meanwhile, the lowest of the low, usually earned half what carpenters were paid, despite the fact that some were educated – a smattering of Greek and Latin was not unknown. John Smith, writing in the first part of the nineteenth century, describes the gardeners at Kew as follows: 'the sons of Gardeners, bailiffs, gamekeepers; and others employed on Noblemen's and Gentlemen's estates, or of farmers and village tradesmen, and a few the youngest sons of clergymen...' The low pay of gardeners was (and is) a familiar complaint. In 1827, in one of Loudon's regular diatribes against Kew, he mentions that 'the journeymen at Kew get only 12 shillings per week, as in public nurseries'. Compare this with the 30 shillings a week, with lodging, that Jane Loudon recommended offering a good gardener. Gardeners' poor pay and conditions were one of the Loudons' recurring themes.

The problem was that there was no regulatory body for gardeners. Anybody could, and did, set himself up as a jobbing gardener, however

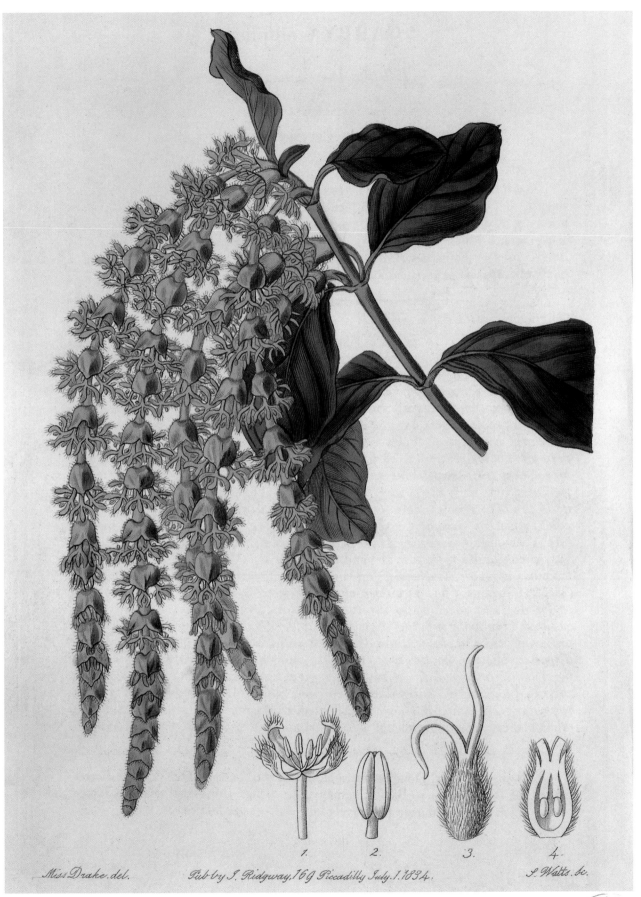

little he knew about the subject. Even experienced gardeners were sometimes reduced to this miserable work. In the 1820s Archibald M'Naughton wrote a memoir in which he described losing his job as a gardener, trying to start a nursery, failing, and having to start work as a jobbing gardener. Three shillings a week was the highest pay he could command, and he was expected to bring his own tools. M'Naughton wrote his account when he was seventy, ill and resigned to spending his final days in the workhouse.

Women probably fared worse. When working women appear in gardens they are weeders. John Loudon describes some on a visit to Alton Towers in Staffordshire and adds: 'On certain occasions these women are put into Swiss dresses, which must add to the singularity of effect.' It must have been a singularly hilarious sight, although forcing estate employees into unusual dress in order to match the landscape also happened elsewhere. Life for the weeders, and for watering boys, must have been dreadful. They found work, and slept, wherever they could.

Even gardeners who were given somewhere to sleep as part of their employment deal were not always much better off. Employed gardeners slept and ate in garden bothies,

some heated, some not. Bothies on well-run estates, and in the gardens of prosperous villas, were little cottages managed by a housekeeper who made the beds, cleaned and made bread. Others were little better than garden sheds, with no table, no real beds and no bedding. Knives, forks, spoons, plates, cups, fuel and candles had to be supplied by the poorly paid gardeners. To keep warm they would sometimes sleep above the boiler rooms on straw pallets...with the obvious danger of fire.

Glasshouses and conservatories were still only found in the richest gardens but, as the

Left: Pineapple pits like this one brought luxury to smart dining tables and misery to those who had to maintain the hot beds round the clock.

century progressed, more and more families acquired them. This meant that gardeners had to be on duty all day every day to care for tender ornamentals and exotics. A mid-century design by the landscape gardener William Miller shows a typical kitchen garden layout. The gardener's house, and the under-gardener's house, took up the same amount of land as the mushroom house, the potting house and the fruit room, and all of them were arranged along the north side of the kitchen garden wall, leaving the warm side for the peach houses, the greenhouse and the vineries. The under-gardener's house was joined to the boiler-room by a door, presumably so that he was close at hand for night-time stoking.

Boilers had to be stoked with back-breaking quantities of coal, and vents and flues had to be opened and shut by hand. Pits of fermenting manure, ground oak bark or elm sawdust (depending on what was available) were a valuable heat source in which to grow pineapples and other exotics, or to produce early peas or salads in winter. These pits could cool off – or ferment up to 30° C – if they were not tended and turned constantly. A twelve-hour day was not unusual, with one hour for lunch and one for breakfast. During the winter, jobs such as potting and cleaning continued by candlelight – and the demands of the plants had to be met even on Christmas Day. Fruit and vegetables had to be forced for the house, and all fruit had to appear in a state of perfection – in the case of pears this sometimes meant wrapping each fruit, still on the tree, with a 'piece of bunting', which, according to Cobbett, 'is a very troublesome, but a very effectual, method'. The soil was another source of labour – tons of readily available manure was worked into it every year.

Boys put up with the rigours of the life either because they were born to it and had little choice or, presumably, in the hope of being able to make the grade as a prosperous head gardener. In some gardens apprentices had to agree to pay the head gardener about half their meagre wages in order to get a job in the first place. Even then, head gardeners could fine apprentices if they left the bothy with the wrong tools, or if they were found chattering.

This tough life was made all the more dreadful by the lethal chemicals that were part of every working day, as we shall see in the following chapter.

Gardeners' working conditions were a constant theme for Loudon, who urged garden owners to provide warmed sheds for their gardeners – and to supply them with decent clothing. He went further and offered a copy of his *Hortus Britannicus* to the first head gardener in England who supplied their men with 'sabots'. These were clog-type overshoes, bought from the Continent, that kept the men's feet warm. However, even Loudon seems to think nothing of having a gardener on call twenty-four hours a day, and he writes warmly about such an arrangement at Stroud House (between Stroud and Haslemere in Surrey). The owners placed a bell over the poor gardener's bedhead, connected by a wire to a pull in the main house, so that the gardener (or his wife, who was presumably employed in the house – this was the usual arrangement) could be called 'for any domestic purpose' or should there be any break-in or disturbance.

Enter the Lawnmower

There was one area of work that became easier for nineteenth-century gardeners – mowing. Lawns created the all-important background for flowering plants, and in flower gardens they were mown by scythe. This was skilled work, as Cobbett states: 'A good short-grass mower is a really able workman...it is quite surprising how close a scythe will go if in a hand that knows how to whet it and use it.'

In 1830 came the invention that would, very gradually, make the scythe redundant. Mr Edwin Budding created the first automated mower. Loudon tested one of the earliest at London Zoo in 1831 and, as always, did so with the gardener's lot in mind. In his report Loudon 'rejoices' that gardeners will be 'emancipated' from mowing either very early or very late in the day because the grass has to be dry for the machine to operate correctly. The new mower may have been marginally easier on the arms than a scythe, but it was heavy work. On larger machines a gardener needed the help of a boy to move it. The gardener would push and the boy would pull, using a handle that reached forward from the centre of the machine. India rubber was added to the moving parts (to make the machinery quieter) and, eventually, a clutch and a collection box, which made the machine similar to today's cylinder mowers.

During the 1830s, however, automated mowers remained the exception rather than

Above: Loudon was commissioned to design Derby Arboretum by a Mr Strutt. Costs were kept low by planting the 11 acres with trees hardy in Derbyshire. In his opening address in 1840, Mr Strutt hoped the park would be used for 'athletic sports and pastimes'.

the rule – so the lawn stayed a velvet monochrome for a few years more until stripes become de rigueur for every fashionable garden.

Larger gardens called for a more extreme mowing solution, and this appeared in the form of horse-drawn mowing machines. Horses' hoofs were clamped into leather 'lawn shoes', to protect the lawn, in a system that survived, at Kew at any rate, until 1961!

Movers and Shakers

From mowers to model farms, John Loudon always seemed to have a contribution to make. His life was mind-bogglingly productive, despite illness, the amputation of an arm and addiction to laudanum (a pain killer made from opium). He published about 60 million words on gardening, architecture and farming. John and his wife Jane can in some ways be called the parents of modern garden publishing.

Their *Gardener's Magazine*, along with authoritative books, such as *The Encyclopaedia of Gardening*, all aimed to bring gardening and garden design, if not to the common man and woman, at least to a wider circle outside the landed gentry and aristocracy. They were great campaigners on issues ranging from prison reform to the creation of half-mile-wide 'breathing zones' between one-mile stretches of development in London.

Loudon's ideas were profoundly influential. By the 1830s his public influence extended far beyond the page when he designed Britain's first public parks – the Terrace Garden in Gravesend and the Derby Arboretum. The eleven-acre Derby Arboretum, which opened in 1840, included 1,000 newly planted trees, many raised on two or three metres high mounds to compensate for the relatively flat site. In the educational spirit of the time, each tree was labelled.

One of the men who helped Loudon on his way to fame and influence was Sir Joseph Banks. It was at Banks's Soho Square house that Loudon met 'most of the eminent scientific men of the day'. Like Loudon, Banks was an important figure in the garden world and, without him, I doubt whether the Horticultural Society would have been formed. He was president of the Royal Society, Kew's de facto first director and a rich, attractive, self-taught botanist with boundless energy and enthusiasm. Banks forked out £10,000 to cover his own passage on Captain Cook's HMS *Endeavour*, plus that of two painters and a draftsman, and an array of up-to-the-minute nets and observation and preservation equipment. A year after his return, in 1772, the King made him Adviser on the Plant Life of the Dependencies. Most of Banks's introductions from the voyage went to Kew. Lava ballast from the voyage went to form the rock garden in the Chelsea Physic Garden and the structure for a moss garden at Kew. Banks's herbarium in Soho Square was open to scholars, and his letter-writing keeps archivists busy today.

On Saturday afternoons the King would walk with Banks at Kew. Royal favour probably made Banks's plans, both for a horticultural society and for Kew, all the easier to fulfil.

Several people had been trying to form a horticultural society since 1800, but it took a flurry of letters from Banks to make it happen. When the seven founders met at Mr Hatchard's rooms their backgrounds and skills reflected the mix of amateur and professional gardeners that can still be found in today's Society.

The men who founded the society, alongside Sir Joseph Banks, were as follows: *John Wedgwood*, son of Josiah the great industrialist, one of the first to suggest beginning a horticultural society. *William Forsyth*, George III's gardener, after whom forsythia is named. He was also a well-known 'fruit-improver' and wrote popular books on training and pruning. *Richard Salisbury*, the botanist and gardener, who pioneered the cultivation of the newly introduced dahlia and was one of the first fellows of the Linnaean Society. *Charles Greville*, MP, a friend of Banks, who developed Milford Haven docks, collected minerals and gardened in Paddington. *James Dickson*, the garden contractor, who probably had a nursery in Croydon and certainly had a seed shop in Covent Garden, having started life as a gardener in the Borders. *William Townsend Aiton*, the first William Aiton's son, who was born at Kew, where he became Royal Gardener, and designed gardens for George IV at Windsor Castle and Brighton Pavilion.

Their meeting at Hatchards marked the start of two centuries of British garden making that would influence the Western world.

Above: Sir Joseph Banks, the national hero we forgot; painted here by Sir Joshua Reynolds. He made Kew the engine house of the Empire and catalysed the creation of the Horticultural Society.

2 Victoriana Gloriosa
Mid Nineteenth-century Razzle-dazzle

Opposite: Victorians said it with flowers – thousands of them – to signal a healthy bank balance. Waddesdon's bedding schemes were sometimes changed three times a year.

Public parks today display versions of Victorian bedding in all their gaudy glory. They're easy to mock – but imagine a park glowing with pristine reds, yellows, blues and purples after the filth, fog and stench of a street in nineteenth-century Liverpool or London. The bedding schemes must have seemed magical. And, in a way, they were. Using easily propagated tender new arrivals – pelargoniums, verbenas, calceolarias, dahlias and more – gardeners would mass plants into colour-coded patterns. The skill and labour involved were tremendous.

1837
Victoria comes to the throne, aged 18, with dominion over New Zealand, and parts of Australia, North America, India, Africa, South America and the Far East.
Charles Barry and Augustus Pugin begin rebuilding the Houses of Parliament in Gothic style

1830s
Wardian case transforms the survival rates of introduced plants

1838
People's Charter demands votes for all men

1840
Queen Victoria marries Prince Albert
Jane Loudon's *Gardening for Ladies* published

Biddulph Grange gardens begin to be constructed

1843
John Loudon dies
Gertrude Jekyll is born
Robert Fortune plant hunts in China
Veitch & Sons nursery sells seeds of monkey puzzle tree recently collected by William Lobb

1844
Battersea Park under construction
Robert Fortune introduces *Anemone japonica, Forsythia viridissima* and *Jasminum nudiflorum*

1844–8
Kew's Palm House built

1845
Irish potato famine
Glass tax abolished

*Opposite: Sir Charles Barry's
Italianate gardens at
Shrubland were a temple to
bedding out. By the late
nineteenth century it was
still trailblazing in design
circles when William
Robinson added a 'wild'
planting scheme.*

The vogue for massed bedding probably originated at Dropmore in Buckinghamshire in the late 1820s and took off at great country estates, such as Shrubland Park in Suffolk. By 1838 no fashionable garden could be without its bedding, as the great gardener, engineer and writer Joseph Paxton noted when he wrote that 'modern flower gardens' were made up of several small, mass-planted beds instead of one large bed containing a variety of plants. Massed they certainly were. There was a contemporary saying that rich people displayed their wealth via their bedding plant requirements – 10,000 for a squire; 20,000 for a baronet; 30,000 for an earl and 40,000 for a duke. There were exceptions to the social rank/bedding plant ratio rule. The Duke of Sutherland's garden, Trentham Park in Staffordshire, needed 100,000 plants a year to sustain the vast formal gardens, which included a 'rivulet' of forget-me-nots. And at Baron Ferdinand de Rothschild's garden, Waddesdon Manor in Buckinghamshire, the bedding was sometimes changed three times a season. Since Waddesdon's restoration, at the end of the twentieth century, the parterres have been laid out using 'computer-grown' blocks of plants slotted into place en masse, whereas in the nineteenth century gardeners faced the back-breaking process of planting every specimen individually. ('Computer

growing' plants is a fairly recent development – a form of planting by numbers, whereby the quantity of plants needed for a display bed is calculated by a computer program and then grown in trays. These plants are laid out in the trays according to the design, so they are ready to go straight into the beds and there is no need to plant each specimen individually, a bit like a jigsaw puzzle.)

Bedding theme variations abounded. Rainbows, both ethereal and earthbound, were all the rage in the mid century, inspired by the garden at Enville Hall, Staffordshire, where a great jet near some of the complex formal gardens created rainbows as it played. In the 1850s George Flemming, head gardener of neighbouring Trentham Park, developed a 'rainbow walk': 'two beds, divided by a gravel walk, in a direct line 200 yards long, slope gently towards the river; each, about 9 feet wide, planted with flowers to represent the colours of the rainbow.'

Flemming also popularized ribbon planting – parallel strips of bedding that could be laid out in straight or serpentine patterns. Many public parks had three strips in patriotic red, white and blue. Promenade-style bedding had 'ribbons' lining either side of a walk, while the wheel style involved concentric bands of

1859

Karl Marx moves to London, having completed the *Communist Manifesto* (1849)

1860s

60 per cent of the country's export trade comes from textiles and, on the land, more food is produced by fewer people thanks to steam engines.

1861

Horticultural Society becomes Royal Horticultural Society and opens its Kensington garden

Prince Albert dies

1862

Plastic invented and showcased at the Great International Exhibition beside the RHS Kensington Gardens

1863

Public hangings abolished

Football Association founded

1864

Hilliers nursery founded in Winchester

1869

Suez canal opens

colour around a mound – a style launched at the Crystal Palace's Rose Mount. With the wisdom of hindsight, Gertrude Jekyll describes ribbons as bedding's '...worst form of all...generally a line of scarlet geranium at the back, then a line of calceolaria, then a line of blue lobelia, and lastly, a line of the inevitable golden feather feverfew... Could anything be more tedious and more stupid? And the ribbon border was at its worst when the lines were not straight, but waved about in weak and silly sinuations.'

Bed shapes, as well as the colours they displayed, became a fashionable fixation. In the 1840s, in particular, contemporary gardening books illustrated and discussed an increasingly wide and controversial range of flower-bed shapes: tears, amoebas, kidneys, commas...think of a shape and it became a bed.

Carpet or mosaic bedding became the vogue in the 1860s, using low-growing, densely planted foliage plants, such as echeveria, sempervivum, arabis and iresine, to form a seamless carpet effect. Some densely packed bedding schemes traced the outlines of monograms and initials. One bedding design even achieved a sort of *trompe l'oeil* effect in which a bed appeared oval when seen from the house, and circular when seen from below.

Meanwhile, at the Crystal Palace's new home in south London, 'Zoomorphic beds' depicted morphologically accurate butterflies.

Colour Theory

These raucous colour schemes would have been anathema in the eighteenth century. In those days colour – a far more subdued spectrum than the newly introduced plants offered – had to be enjoyed in the privacy of walled gardens. But, by the mid nineteenth century, colour acquired status with the publication of Johann Goethe's *Theory of Colours*, which categorized it in a spectrum from cold blue to warm orange. Colour gained added respectability when Victorians reminded themselves that Ancient Greek statues were painted, as were medieval churches.

Inside houses colour became more vibrant, with the use of aniline dyes and new pigments such as cobalt blue. Gardens had to match this glorious kaleidoscope. Clashing plant colours were popular. For instance, the ubiquitous *Pelargonium* 'Mrs Pollock' had bright scarlet flowers and yellow leaves patched green in the centre and topped with a red ring.

Head gardeners and gardening journalists (many were one and the same thing) competed to come up with new ways of displaying all these colourful plants. One was the 'shot silk effect' created by planting a mass of one colour and enhancing it by slight variations – *Verbena venosa* (now *V. rigida*) planted with *Pelargonium* 'Old Scarlet' for instance. One expert wrote that oranges and reds, blues and lilacs must never appear together, but orange and purple, yellow and blue, blue and white, red and blue would always contrast well. Some head gardeners recommended that colour schemes be tried at different times of day to allow for the Purkinje effect of red receding and blue appearing as light fades. David Thomson's book, *The Handy Book of the Flower Garden* (1868), suggested trying out real flower colours – by scattering petals – on planting plans where lawns and other background colours had been painted.

There was an underlying problem with all colour theory, however: one gardener's carmine was another gardener's red – in other words there was no authoritative standardization of plant colour. Plant names themselves didn't help because, as the Royal Horticultural Society was to discover later in the century, plants were often misnamed and, anyway, a 'purple verbena' could indicate a number of different colours. It was not until 1938 that flower colours were standardized in a chart designed by the Royal Horticultural Society.

Above: Garish plants like Pelargonium 'Mrs Pollock'. were ideal for bedding out. Even the leaves joined in the cacophany of clashing colours.

Beyond Bedding

Whatever the colour schemes, traditional bedding displays had a short season. So the season was extended by bulbs at one end of the year, and dahlias and chrysanthemums at the other. The chrysanthemum craze was started in 1855 at the Inner Temple in London, where chrysanthemums took to the stage as soon as the roses went over. Evergreen winter gardens were already known, but acquired added allure with their new name, 'winter bedding', which covered plants such as gaultheria, hollies, skimmia and mahonia.

Not that Victorian gardens were simply variations on the bedding theme. In 1846

Right: Arley Hall's renowned double herbaceous borders date back to the first half of the nineteenth century. These borders are living proof that herbaceous plants never completely left the garden, despite the bedding vogue.

Above: Joseph Paxton, the gardener who became a knight, was renowned as an engineer, plantsman and innovator. He designed and controlled the construction of the Crystal Palace (opposite) – the pre-fab building that predicted the modern movement.

Arley Hall had vast, double herbaceous borders, and one head gardener wrote in 1859: 'A garden without a border for mixed flowers is seldom to be met with.'

Most gardens also featured an orchard, a productive kitchen garden and a mass of different ornamental plants. Ferns had become increasingly popular from the late 1830s, when James Bateman, an early vice-president of the Horticultural Society, made a fernery at Biddulph Grange, Staffordshire. Wisteria became the 'in' plant of the 1860s, when Robert Fortune's cultivars arrived from Japan. Sitka spruces, monkey puzzles, and the first Wellingtonias and redwoods of California were a 'must' for larger gardens, which often included pinetums and 'American gardens', usually meaning an area of ericaceous trees and shrubs. Roses were popular, too, as you can see at Warwick Castle's rosarium, restored in 1986 to an 1877 design by Robert Marnock, the landscaper and curator of the Royal Botanical Society's garden in Regent's Park.

The obsession with flowers of almost every kind spread indoors. Glass cases extended the life of house-plants, which were once short-lived victims of fumes from coal fires and gas and oil lamps. Living plants aside, flowers had insinuated themselves into every aspect of life.

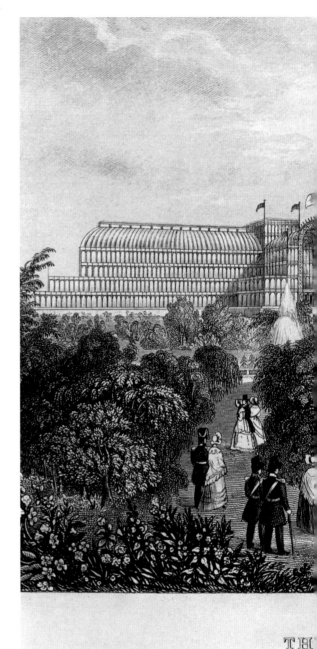

Flower-painted china, convolvulus lamp stands, fuchsia curtain hooks, thistle inkstands and floral broaches ensured year-round floral decoration and triggered a heated debate about whether nature should be imitated – or interpreted – by art.

Joseph Paxton

Flowers in art had their place, but living plants commanded the greatest prestige and

EW CRYSTAL PALACE AT SYDENHAM.

made head gardeners all powerful. They ruled estates and often overruled the owners, who would bow to the whims of these green-fingered potentates. With the backing of a benevolent employer, a talented head gardener could become a household name, as Joseph Paxton demonstrated. He began work as a gardener and, within a couple of decades, had been knighted, founded two magazines and designed the Crystal Palace.

The Bedfordshire boy was foreman of the Horticultural Society gardens in Chiswick until 1826, when the Duke of Devonshire, who had leased his London garden to the Society, appointed Paxton as head gardener at Chatsworth in Derbyshire. Paxton arrived at 4.30 a.m. on a May morning, climbed over a garden wall, inspected the gardens and, when the men arrived at 6 a.m., ordered the waterworks to be turned on. Breakfast with

Above: Paxton's
conservatory, the 'Great
Stove', at Chatsworth,
housed the first giant water
lily (opposite) to flower in
Europe. Punch magazine
immortalized the events as
follows: 'On unbent leaf,
in fairy guise / Reflected in
the water / Beloved, admired
by hearts and eyes / Stands
Annie Paxton's daughter.'

was essentially pre-fab, too) and created the 277ft long conservatory at Chatsworth that Albert and Victoria visited in December 1843.

Conservatories became increasingly popular from the mid century because the glass tax and brick tax were repealed. Better still, the price of coal began to fall. Two inventions made glasshouses all the more attractive: wrought iron, which took the place of wood (so letting in more light because glazing bars could be thin and strong); and improved sheet glass, which was more stable and larger than earlier versions. In fact, wood came back into fashion because it was less likely to contract violently and break the glass than iron and, as Paxton's (originally Loudon's) ridge-and-furrow system demonstrated, wooden frames could still let in plenty of light.

In 1849 Paxton became the first person in Europe to get the monumental water lily *Victoria amazonica* to flower – having designed and built a conservatory for the plant, inspired by the structure of its massive leaves. But life inside many domestic conservatories was less successful because few understood how to care for tender plants. So, in the words of one contemporary, instead of 'a gay assemblage of luxuriant verdure and blossoms...they are generally

the housekeeper secured his first meeting with his future wife, the housekeeper's niece Sarah Brown. In the years that followed Paxton started the Horticultural Register and became one of his generation's most influential gardeners. While this extra-ordinary Victorian made his fortune as a gardener, conditions for mortal gardeners remained as unpredictable as they were at the start of the century.

Conservatories and Glasshouses

Paxton was a champion of the glasshouse. He invented a sort of pre-fab domestic glasshouse in the 1860s (his design for the Crystal Palace, sketched on blotting paper for Prince Albert,

Above: Kew's glittering Palm House was completed in 1848. Designed by Decimus Burton and Richard Turner, it is 65ft high in places, with a walkway to give visitors a canopy-level view of the exotics.

Opposite: Nelson's victory on the Nile was probably the inspiration for 'Egypt', pictured here. The stone doorway leads through to a revolting squat figure, the ape of Thoth – the Egyptian god of botany's attendant.

filled with sickly naked plants in peat soil, with hard names, which one half of people of taste and fashion, and nine-tenths of mankind in general, care nothing about.' Only the most experienced gardeners could produce the aesthetic and edible paradise promoted by the gardening press, in which palms, agaves, yuccas, camellias, acacias, oranges, tree ferns, birds of paradise and Cape primroses thrived alongside bananas, loquats, mangos, guavas, nutmeg and pimentos.

The need to heat the conservatory produced various ingenious systems of coal-fired or steam-driven heating. The wooden flues were dangerous and dirty – they regularly caught fire. By the middle of the century the old contraptions were beginning to be replaced by circulating hot water systems.

The first free-standing glasshouses had boilers placed at the centre of the building and this acquired a thick layer of soot across their glass. As a result, boiler chimneys were placed away from conservatories. Kew's beautiful Palm House, designed by Decimus Burton with the help of Richard Turner, is a case in point – the striking Italianate chimney was sited at the far side of the pond, well away from the glistening house.

Larger conservatories had railways installed on which to move heavy plants and bring in coal. At Cragside in Northumberland the orange and lemon pots also stood on turntables to give them even sunlight.

Glasshouses and conservatories were high-maintenance toys.

Theme Parks

It is tempting to assume that all mid-Victorian gardens were made up of expensive conservatories and bedding displays. In fact, there were one or two remarkably original gardens – and a few that bordered on the weird. Biddulph Grange included an area

Right: This part of 'China' at Biddulph Grange is a temple reached by a winding rock tunnel. The building was probably inspired by Robert Fortune's description of a mandarin's house.

called 'Egypt'. This was made from yew topiary around an Egyptian-style stone portico leading through to the dimly lit stone figure of the Ape of Thoth. Those brave enough to pass the ape turned sharp right and out into a woodland of newly introduced junipers, monkey puzzles, deodars and pines. But when visitors glanced backwards...Egypt had become a wattle-and-daub Cheshire cottage.

This eerie, beautiful landscape was started in about 1840 by James Bateman and his wife Maria Egerton-Warburton. It was created to show off newly introduced specimen plants. 'China', another area of their garden, included

plant hunter Robert Fortune's golden larch, variegated bamboos and *Skimmia japonica*. It was completely hidden from the rest of the garden, and the plants were set off by a joss house, dragons and a gilded water buffalo. There were many more unusual features and plant collections, including a rhododendron ground, a dahlia walk and a stumpery – a display of upended roots.

Down the road at Alton Towers, an almost equally bizarre garden evolved between 1814 and 1860. A vast pagoda fountain erupted into a landscape with a Swiss cottage (made for a blind harpist), grand conservatories packed

with palms and exotics and 'Stone Henge', a double-decker construction of monoliths.

This eclectic mixture of styles became known as 'gardenesque' thanks to Edward Kemp's book *How to Lay out a Small Garden*, which appeared in 1850. The term had first been used by Loudon in 1832 to describe a garden in which each plant was arranged singly to display its full potential. In Kemp's book, however, the expression applied to garden layout, rather than planting, referring to a random mixture of styles without any unifying theme, and it was Kemp's use of the word that caught on.

Mellor's Garden near Macclesfield, in Cheshire, may not have been Gardenesque, but it was certainly unusual. This mid century landscape by James Mellor, the son of a mill owner, was a three-acre allegory of *The Pilgrim's Progress* complete with 'Hell', where the stench of sulphur and the howl of Aeolian harps would emanate when visitors were around.

These gardens were exceptions. Mainstream garden design was 'Italianate' because the style was considered the best way to display bedding. 'Italianate' came to mean terraces, flights of steps, fountains, balustrades and symmetrical flower-beds, although it covered a multitude of styles from many periods as well as places – Dutch formal, French rococo, Islamic gardens and Elizabethan and Jacobean knot gardens. The chief proponent of Italianate landscaping was Sir Charles Barry, architect of the Houses of Parliament, who created gardens at Trentham Hall, Shrubland Park and Cliveden in Buckinghamshire.

High Adventure

Plants could bring as much kudos to a garden owner as grand and expensive hard landscaping schemes like Barry's. Plant hunters scoured the world for trophies to please their sponsors – and recorded every frisson of danger to please their public. High adventure was a crucial part of the package – the nineteenth-century equivalent of a merchandising opportunity, and one that sometimes cost plant hunters their lives. A successful book would top up the plant hunters' meagre pay and ensure future sponsorship. Achieving the right balance between botany and adventure was not easy. As Reginald Farrer pointed out, in the early twentieth century, some people loved the adventure and hated the botany, while with others it was the reverse. Farrer also commented bitterly that by the time he was plant hunting, new material was difficult to

find. He had every right to be envious of the Kew plant hunter Richard Oldham, who described his method of plant collecting in the Orient:

...the ONLY way of botanizing well in the south of Japan, is to take rooms or a house, get 2 or 3 assistants, instruct them how to help you, & when the most intelligent of them understands the work, get a passport for him from the Customs House, provide him with money, paper etc. & send him into the interior, trusting him to select the best localities, pay his expenses as he goes, & let him bring home his collections on pack horses or in the best way he can.

In the same year the Horticultural Society commissioned Robert Fortune to go to China to find a tree which produced two-pound peaches; a double yellow rose; a plant that made rice paper, as well as blue peonies – a tall order. Reluctantly, they allowed him to take a gun, although they felt a club alone was more appropriate. On the journey there, Fortune, who had started as an apprentice in Scotland before running the Chiswick hothouses, was attacked by thieves and also suffered various illnesses. To begin with, he was not impressed with the flora. Then he went to Chusan island:

I have met here, for the first time, the beautiful wisteria wild on the hills, where it climbs among the hedges and on the trees, and its flowering branches hang in graceful festoons by the side of the narrow roads which lead over the mountains ... azaleas ... abound on the hillsides of this island ... few can form any idea of the gorgeous and striking beauty of these azalea-clad mountains...clematises, and a hundred others, mingle their flowers with them, and make us confess that China is indeed the 'central flowery land'.

As the local people became less suspicious of him, he visited nurseries for plants – but his heart was stolen by the tradition of planting flowers on graves.

When I first discovered *Anemone japonica*, it was in full flower among the graves of the natives, which are found in the ramparts of Shanhae; it blooms in November, when other flowers have gone by, and is a most appropriate ornament to the last resting place of the dead ...

He returned with the 'Japanese' anemone, white wisteria, weigela, winter-flowering honeysuckles and more.

Chemical Warfare

The explosion of 'new' plants brought with it the inevitable problem of pest and disease control. It was exacerbated by the vogue for mass planting, which left bedding displays vulnerable – one pest could wipe out a whole section of a display.

Science offered a solution – at a price. Victorian gardening manuals read like a chemical version of *The Water Babies*. Mind-blowing chemicals were part of the gardener's everyday arsenal and included arsenic, strychnine, nicotine, mercury (mixed with soft soap against mealy bugs on pineapples), quicklime and sulphur. Gardeners handled garden chemicals without protection and were expected to make chlorine gas – to protect potatoes from 'murrain' (probably blight) – by mixing vitriol, manganese dioxide and salt. Paris green (arsenic mixed with copper) was also used on potato crops. The gardener put the mixture into a box on a stick and wafted the toxic green powder over the vegetable garden.

Experiments on agricultural chemicals began in the 1840s. At Kew, investigations began of plant pests and diseases in 1875, but the harmful side-effects of garden chemicals were not the focus of research. Most people knew that arsenic and so on were poisons, but few seemed to realize the dangers they posed to those who worked with them (after all, small quantities of arsenic were being used in various medicines until the 1930s). In the second half of the nineteenth century Shirley Hibberd, editor of *Amateur Gardening* and author of many manuals, recommended countless chemical remedies, including: Fowler's Insecticide (Potassium arsenate, a form of arsenic); fumigation with tobacco; phosphor paste; sulphur; Gishurst Compound and McDonald's Liquid Insecticide. An engraving of a gardener using the last of these shows him dipping plants into a half barrel of the stuff with bare hands and no eye protection.

Fumigation was a source of great debate. 'Tobacco paper' and 'tobacco rag' – brown paper and hessian soaked in nicotine solution and dried with saltpetre – were lit and left to smoulder and release their toxic fumes around aphid-infested plants. Hibberd showed great concern about the safety of fumigation. This seems an enlightened view until it becomes clear that he is concerned for the plant rather than the gardener. Fumigation spawned a mass of products: Corry's Lethorian Cones, which looked like cone-shaped fireworks; Campbell's Fumigating Insecticide Rolls; little

NO MORE WEEDS
THE CELEBRATED
ACME WEED KILLER

AS USED IN THE
CRYSTAL PALACE GROUNDS

PERMANENTLY DESTROYS WEEDS,
MOSS &c ON GARDEN WALKS, DRIVES &c.
NO SMELL   CLEANSES THE GRAVEL

PROPRIETORS & MANUFACTURERS
THE ACME CHEMICAL COMPY LTD
TUNBRIDGE, KENT & BOLTON, LANCASHIRE.

fumigation stoves – such as Tebb's Universal Fumigator, and hand-held fumigators.

Those who wanted to fumigate a couple of pots inside the house, rather than a whole conservatory, were instructed to hang a sheet between two bentwood chairs and put the plants and fumigator inside. A lady correspondent to a garden magazine went one better – she used a crinoline, sewn up at the waist, as a fumigation tent.

Pest-and disease-fighting tools multiplied. In 1860 Mr Spary of the Queen Graperies, Brighton, invented a Fumigator and Mildew Annihilator and sent it for inspection to the Horticultural Society. The aphis brush was a more familiar aid – a sugar tong structure with brushes or sponges on the pincers. The sponges were usually soaked in insecticide.

There was little distinction between natural and chemical controls. Chemical advice ran alongside advice which would be regarded as 'organic' by gardeners today. For instance, 'Poudrette' – a disgusting but fertile mixture of ash and human waste – was used as soil conditioner. One reader wrote to a journal to say that he used a peewit to peck off 'injurious insects' from 'stove plants'. Another reader maintained that he used a 'mother and two

young hedgehogs' to get rid of woodlice. Hibberd took a more robust approach and recommended stamping on slugs and snails.

But it wasn't only chemicals that the Victorians enlisted in their quest for better, more efficient gardening.

Inventions – the Wardian Case

Of the plants introduced to Britain in the eighteenth and early nineteenth centuries, only a tiny proportion survived. Most died in transit and many of the rest died through ignorance because, even at Kew, gardeners had no way of knowing how to care for many 'new' plants.

Dr Nathaniel Bagshaw Ward transformed plant survival rates with his glass plant case. Invented around 1830, it created an ecosystem and protected plants from extremes of weather and the salt air on the voyage home. Until then plants had been packed in a variety of ways, some more logical than others. They were stored in converted barrels or stuffed into split bamboo canes and sealed with waxed cloth and mud; or they were wrapped into rubber sheets and stored in the ship's ice rooms or water tanks; or they were parcelled into waxed cloth, which was then covered in layers of soap. Only the most robust could survive.

Dr Ward's invention, known as the Wardian case, was so successful that it continued to be used by Kew until the 1960s, while domestic gardeners used versions of the Wardian case to display plants inside the house.

There were other inventions that had direct impact on the domestic garden. Secateurs, originally designed for vineyard work, were dreamt up by one Bertrand de Moleville, who narrowly escaped death in the French Revolution. Garden twine, made from jute, was invented by George Acland. He brought it back from Bengal to Dundee in 1828 and added creosote (to prevent rotting), so giving twine its familiar colour. Rubberized hose-pipes came on to the market in the 1850s,

gradually replacing the leather ones. These highly practical inventions were followed by more esoteric items, such as hail protectors and 'Sangster's Florumbra', a plant umbrella designed to be screwed into position on a pole beside the plant.

Public Parks

The Victorian thirst for invention and innovation went far beyond scientific ingenuity, and into park and garden design itself. When F. L. Olmsted, designer of Central Park in New York and the 'Emerald Necklace' of parks in Boston, visited Paxton's recently opened Birkenhead Park in Liverpool in 1850 he commented: '...the privileges of the garden were enjoyed equally by all classes...in

Above: Wardian cases like this were used at Kew until the 1960s. When they were invented over a century earlier, newly discovered plants finally had a fighting chance of survival on the long voyage back to Britain.

democratic America there is nothing to be thought of as comparable with this People's Garden ...'

The new public parks were remarkable and a far cry from eighteenth-century pleasure gardens, such as Vauxhall and Cremorne. Old-style pleasure gardens were a cross between open-air nightclubs and freak shows – they 'exhibited' Siamese twins, and had dancing stages, orchestras and lighting. The new parks were designed to educate. The Crystal Palace's grounds included prehistoric monsters roaming around scenes from our supposed geological past, and a model of a Derbyshire open pit mine. Victoria Park, designed by John Nash's pupil James Pennethorne in 1840, had a pagoda on an island and some of the most renowned bedding displays in London.

Gardens and gardening were seen as routes to betterment. Florists' societies ran competitions to, 'lift [cottagers] out of the

degrading habits of sluggish pauperism', and public parks were designed to give visitors fresh air, education and a taste for wholesome gardening.

Not that every park was founded on philanthropic ideals. Battersea, for example, was a developer's dream. It was a builder, Thomas Cubitt, who first suggested a Regent's Park-style creation on what was, in 1844, a riverside meadow with Sunday fairs and a notorious reputation. In order to shore up three-quarters of a mile of riverside and raise it by 24ft, 750,000 cubic yards of earth, subsoil and rubble moved to Battersea from the Surrey docks. The newly elevated 200 acres was then moulded into a basic plan mapped out by James Pennethorne with five miles of path and carriage drive, a 22-acre lake and a half-mile elm avenue. One outstanding feature was James Pulham's rockwork. 'Pulhamite' rock gardens, some of which were remarkably lifelike imitations of rock, made from Portland cement sometimes mixed with fossils and laid, in strata, over a clinker framework.

Provincial centres had parks, too. In 1846 Cambridge Botanic Garden moved from a small site in the city to forty acres outside it, where 'respectably dressed strangers' were allowed to visit. Naturally, the garden aimed to be educational and the beds were laid out to illustrate the latest plant classifications. The present curator, John Parker, reckons that all the trees in the arboretum were planted to show variation in species. For instance, two black pines planted close together show genetic variation due to mutation: the Austrian specimen has sloping branches so that snow falls off without breaking them; the Spanish specimen has spreading branches. The garden was popular in the nineteenth century, especially when it had added attractions – notably a tightrope walker who brought in a record two and a half thousand visitors in one day.

Garden visiting was certainly popular. Despite Loudon's mixed reviews of Chatsworth, the estate had 48,000 visitors a year by the mid nineteenth century. Kew, which havered between its dual roles as a pleasure garden and a testing station for imperial economic crops, reluctantly let visitors in. In the words of John Lindley, secretary of the Horticultural Society: 'You entered unwelcome, you rambled about suspected, and you were let out with manifest gladness shown at your departure.' By the 1850s, when two new railway stations helped make Kew one of the most popular destinations from the East End, 180,000 visitors a year were pouring in. Visiting hours became less restrictive, and in the 1870s, to the disgust of the director Joseph Hooker, Kew became, in parts at least, the very model of a modern pleasure garden, with calceolarias, verbena, petunias, dwarf dahlias and geraniums.

Whatever the boffins thought of Kew, the public felt ownership, and in 1877 demonstrators marched and waved banners, hoping to get the gardens opened earlier and even to have the high wall along Kew Road taken down.

Kensington Gardens and the RHS

While Kew's historic acres continued to attract the punters, the Horticultural Society, which had once come close to taking over the great botanic garden, was floundering – by the mid century it had borrowed the huge sum of £10,000. Radical action was needed. The society moved out of its first permanent HQ in Regent Street and, more disastrously,

Below: Prince Albert came to
the rescue of the floundering
Horticultural Society in
1859. He gave them funds
from the Great Exhibition
to build the gardens at
Kensington, as well as
bestowing a charter to
make the Society 'Royal'.

sold its library. Still the problems persisted, and the society might have folded if it hadn't been for Prince Albert, whose fascination with horticulture (and reproduction) is recorded in an 1843 cartoon showing the prince lifting cloches, each of which reveals a child: the nurseryman in the background is saying that there are too many of 'that sort o' plants'. The prince recommended leasing land at Kensington Gore for a Horticultural Society garden with a conservatory. At his suggestion, finance came from profits of the 1851 Great Exhibition and from fund raising. The queen, patron of the society, donated £1,000 and added a long list of donations from members of the Royal Family. High society followed her example, the gardens opened in 1861 and the Horticultural Society became the Royal Horticultural Society.

The tunnel that now leads from South Kensington tube station to the Science Museum once opened at the gardens' entrance, and the eastern arcades of the gardens ran down Exhibition Road. Their design was an influential – and controversial – folly of Italianate grandeur, with fountains, an arcade running around the perimeter and a conservatory with a tessellated floor by Minton. Terracotta was used for some of the balustrades and façades of the walls and

Right: Flower power ruled alongside Queen Victoria, whose 1887 Jubilee inspired designs smothered with roses.

buildings, and this triggered a terracotta craze. The first cast-iron bandstand appeared and became the template for bandstands in public parks throughout England. William Nesfield, the painter turned garden designer, and George Eyles (former superintendent of the Crystal Palace) laid out four parterres at the centre of the garden. These depicted a shamrock, a thistle, a leek and a rose in gravel and box. It caused bluster among horticulturalists, who wanted more plants and flowers, but in 1864 alone the gardens attracted 152,962 visitors, paying from 7s 6d on show days to 3d on the queen's birthday and for a few months after the London season. On Sundays the gardens were open to the fellows and their friends '*personally* introduced', as the proceedings state.

The society appeared to prosper – *The Journal* which became today's monthly RHS magazine *The Garden*, was launched in 1866. Two years later the society formed the Lindley Library Trust and began to build a new library based on that bought from its secretary John Lindley. However, the society was living beyond its means. In the 1870s the gardens attempted to increase income: lawn tennis was allowed, although plans for an ice rink were refused. It was no good – the gardens closed and became the site for Imperial College and other great institutions. The Natural History Museum and the Albert Hall had been built during the gardens' lifetime.

All the same, the society continued to reinvent itself and in 1875 it acknowledged that not every garden enthusiast was a landowner or head gardener. At their regular shows, a class was introduced for a selection of flowers displayed within a frame 3.3m square. The idea had been copied from the Lincoln Horticultural Society and was part of a gradual democratization of the society.

Left: Fashionable Victorian dining tables, ballrooms, drawing rooms and hostesses had to be smothered in flowers – the more exotic and complex the arrangement, the better.

Party Party

High society, meanwhile, had no such democratic leanings and instead used gardens as part of the ongoing game of one-upmanship. Horticulture had become haughty culture, and every fashionable hostess had to ensure that she (along with her dining tables, ballrooms and daughters) was festooned with flowers. Status could be clocked up by throwing house parties and balls with lavish displays of exotic fruit and flowers, while out-of-season vegetables grown *in situ* offered proof of an opulent garden run by a top head gardener, no expense spared. After visiting Gunnersbury Park, Benjamin Disraeli wrote effusively to Baroness Charlotte Rothschild, thanking her for a surprise that had been loaded into his carriage while he was dining – a crop of Gunnersbury's famous pineapples. The same hostess often arranged for miniature orange trees, grown at Gunnersbury, to be taken to the family house in Piccadilly so that guests could pick the fruits for themselves.

Ornamental plants were just as important as exotic fruit. Lady Eastlake describes an evening when the *interior* of Devonshire House had been decorated with pyramids of red and white camellias and 'beds' of geraniums and roses. 'The dresses too were beautiful and so fantastic they would have passed for fancy dress a few years ago...head-dresses with long creepers of flowers interwoven with diamonds...'

To set off opulent plant displays Minton, Wedgwood and Doulton created ornate ceramic plant pots and containers, while others were made from silver or gold. Summer parties drifted into gardens lit with flares, Chinese lanterns and 'variegated lamps' to light paths and display lavish flower gardens.

What better way to convey wealth, after all, than with displays of rare flowers and fruits raised in splendid, heated houses that were far better kitted out than most Victorian homes?

3 Floral v Formal

The Battle for the Late Nineteenth-century Garden

Opposite: Renishaw Hall in Derbyshire epitomized the new approach to Italianate formality. Sir George Sitwell, who created the gardens, spent many years in Italy.

At the peak of their formidable power, head gardeners became locked in a power struggle with architects over who should design gardens. The architects – we would now call them landscape architects – felt they had the education and training to make the best of a garden. They maintained that history, particularly the Italian Renaissance, held the answers to contemporary garden design. Head gardeners, on the other hand, felt that they should dictate the shape and form of a garden because they understood plants. The result was described by New York's Central Park designer Frederick Olmsted in 1892 as a 'contradictory hash of formal-natural gardening'. The main protagonists in the struggle were the great Irish garden writer and gardener William Robinson and the architect Sir Reginald Blomfield.

1870
William Robinson's *The Wild Garden* published
'Phyllomania' brings foliage into fashionable gardens

1871
William Morris begins his garden at Kelmscot in Oxfordshire. Arts and Crafts movement in full swing

1872
Claude Monet paints *Impression: Soleil Levant*
Edward Lear's *Nonsense Botany* published

1874
Alchemilla mollis introduced

1876
Alexander Bell patents the telephone

1877
William Morris founds the Society for the Protection of Ancient Buildings

1879
Thomas Edison invents the electric lamp

1885
John Singer Sargent paints *Carnation Lily, Lily Rose*

1886
Karl Benz invents the world's first car

1888
First Leyland cypress seedling discovered, a cross between Monterey cypress and *Chamaecyparis nootkatensis*, introduced 35 years earlier

Sir George Sitwell designs
Renishaw Hall gardens

1892

Reginald Blomfield's *The Formal Garden in England* published

1895

Octavia Hill founds the National Trust

Oscar Wilde sentenced to two years' hard labour at Reading Gaol for a homosexual affair

1896

First women gardeners at Kew

1899

RHS stages the International Hybridization Conference

Aspirin patented and sold to the general public

1900

'Chinese' Wilson introduces *Clematis armandii*

1901

Edward VII comes to the throne

Wilson introduces *Davidia involucrata*, the handkerchief tree

1902

Marconi sends the first transatlantic telegraph

Robinson's prose was charming and persuasive. He started work as a gardener in Ireland and eventually gardened for the publisher John Murray in England. And he just happened to mention to the publisher that his – Robinson's – ideas were so revolutionary that a book had to be written about them. *The Wild Garden*, published by John Murray in 1870, recommended informal plantings of bulbs and herbaceous plants in place of regimented bedding schemes. Robinson's ideas were not nearly as revolutionary as he liked to make out, but the vigour and clarity of his writing won a wide audience. He lashed out against the increasingly popular vogue for statues as 'ugly extravagances' that were bad enough in private gardens, but in public gardens were 'hurtful to the public taste'. And he was critical of Italianate style in general: 'It was said that none but an Italian garden would suit South Kensington...the result...was miserable,' he wrote, echoing a common complaint against the RHS gardens that they exhibited too much structure and too few plants.

Herbaceous plantings, an important part of Robinson's 'new' approach, had never left the scene – they usually co-existed with dazzling, mid century bedding displays. In the Royal Botanic Garden at Regent's Park, herbaceous plantings had been centre stage since the mid nineteenth century thanks to Robert Marnock, who was experimenting with herbaceous plants when a young gardener called Robinson arrived to help. By that time the cognoscenti regarded bedding as passé, and writers such as Shirley Hibberd were commending herbaceous plantings to replace bedding. *The Wild Garden* appeared in the wake of the herbaceous revival, but Robinson, an inveterate networker and an occasional correspondent of *The Times*, popularized the herbaceous theme with his books and his magazine, *The Garden*.

He sweetened his propaganda by suggesting cost-saving as well as fashionable ideas: he recommended hedges instead of iron fences, plants that looked after themselves once established, and less frequent mowing. 'Who would not rather see the waving grass with countless flowers than a close surface without a blossom?' he demanded. He told his readers to plant snowdrops, anemones, grape hyacinths, dog tooth violets and *Tulipa sylvestris* in areas of rough grass.

In 1885 he bought Gravetye Manor in Sussex, where he put into practice many of his planting ideas. According to Dame Sylvia Crowe, one of the great landscape architects of the twentieth century, the meadow sloping in front of Robinson's house contained 'tulip and anemone species seldom seen elsewhere.'

Into this bucolic scene strode Sir Reginald Blomfield, whose book, *The Formal Garden in England*, was published in 1892. Unlike Robinson, who delivered his message in appropriately flowery prose, Blomfield took the storm trooper approach. Here is his opinion of Britain's most famous eighteenth-century landscaper: '"Capability" Brown... began as a kitchen gardener, but took the judicious line that knowledge hampered originality. He accordingly dispensed with any training in design, and rapidly rose to eminence.' Ouch!

Blomfield moved on to attack Robinson, alleging, among other things, that all

Opposite: William Robinson was a great propagandist against bedding and for bulbs and herbaceous plants. His garden at Gravetye (the meadow in front of his house is shown above) became a palette for his theories.

Opposite: Reginald
Blomfield favoured formality
like that of Renishaw.
Protracted mud-slinging
between Blomfield and
Robinson caused a sensation
among gardeners and chaos
in gardens: which style was
correct – formal or flowery?

1902–4

Pablo Picasso's 'Blue period'

1903

Grey squirrels introduced to
Britain at Kew Gardens

Wisley given to the RHS

Wright brothers launch the
world's first true aeroplane

1904

George Forrest's first expedition
to China

1905

Emmeline Pankhurst founds the
Women's Social & Political Union

First Russian Revolution

Wilson introduces the regal lily

1906

Lawrence Johnston begins the
garden at Hidcote

1908

Henry Ford produces the Model T,
the first relatively affordable car

Kew Gardens advertised on
London Underground

Wilson introduces *Magnolia
sinensis*

1910

George V comes to the throne

1912

Reginald Farrer starts writing
The English Rock Garden

1913

George Bernard Shaw's Eliza
selling hybridized violets and
learning about class structure in
Pygmalion, the play that inspired
My Fair Lady

The Chelsea Flower Show begins

1914

First World War begins

Robinson's ideas derived from the Great
Exhibition of 1851. As far as Blomfield was
concerned, the head gardener should know his
place: 'The horticulturalist and the gardener
are indispensable, but they should work under
control' – and that control belonged, in
Blomfield's eyes, to architects like himself.

He trampled through the bedding-out system
and explained that gardens should emulate
the architectural style of the house, just as
William Morris had suggested. This was
hardly a new idea but, like Robinson and his
pro-herbaceous stance, Blomfield served up
'his' idea as if it were a departure. In fact, the
two men had other things in common, not
least their highly public dislike for bedding
out, doomed anyway by disease in calceolaria
and verbena stock, devastating late frosts and
gloomy summers in the latter part of the
century.

Blomfield was not alone on his 'Italianate'
terrace of ideas. There was Inigo Triggs, who
formed a contemporary catalogue of formal
features in his book *Formal Gardens in England
and Scotland*. Formalism was also espoused by
many of the great designers of the day,
including Harold Peto and Sir George Sitwell,
who created his version of an Italian
Renaissance garden at Renishaw in

Derbyshire. In Wales Sir Clough Williams-
Ellis, Portmeirion's architect, gave a twist to
contemporary formalism with his blue-and-
gold painted gates. At Bodnant, Lord
Aberconway installed traditional Italianate
terraces.

Despite the irreconcilable differences between
formal and informal garden styles, they
sometimes lived side by side. The mid century
temple to bedding out and Italianate
architecture, Shrubland Park in East Anglia,
employed Robinson to add a 'wild side' to the
planting. Robinson's record of his work leaves
the impression that the whole of Shrubland
Park's formality was ripped out in favour of
'natural' planting. Not so. But his description
is illuminating about both styles:

Shrubland Park, in Suffolk, illustrates the
recent history of English flower-gardening...
The great terrace in front of the house was laid
out in scrolls and intricate beds, all filled with
plants of a few decided colours, principally
red, white and blue, and edged with Box...not a
creeper was permitted to ramble over the
masonry and stonework...Every bit of ivy that
tried to creep up the walls and cover the
stonework had to be removed, to leave the
stone in its first bareness. Where some
particular colour was wanted in a certain spot,

coloured stones were freely used – yellow, red and blue – and in the summer, when the hedgerows and meadows are full of flowers, there were no flowers in this large garden to cut for the house! A few years ago the elaborate designs were swept away, and the terrace garden planted with the flowers everyone loves – Roses, Lavender... One of the most interesting spots of Shrubland is the Bamboo walk, a straight walk, planted at one time with smooth ribbon borders. These were swept away, and the Bamboo and tall Lilies now fill their place... [along with] the Plume Poppy...Lilies; Funkias, or Plantain Lilies and Evening Primroses.

The debate about formal and 'wild' gardens helps explain the eclecticism in gardens around the turn of the century. For thirty or forty years bedding had been the clear fashion statement in the main garden, whatever happened around the perimeter. Now that there was no consensus, all kinds of influences crept into the garden. Japanese features became increasingly popular; alpine plants, introduced by Farrer and others, made rock gardens desirable features; nostalgia for a largely imagined past of cottage gardens were extolled by the Pre-Raphaelites and others, and an increasing number of hybrid roses made rose gardens fashionable. The Rev. Henry T.

Ellacombe's book, *The Plant-Lore and Garden-Craft of Shakespeare*, brought Shakespeare's plants and words into the garden. Religious texts also found their way in – one Wigtownshire garden used box trees to 'write' a phrase from Psalm 103.

The ideas that Blomfield and Robinson represented were to persist in rivalry in the twentieth century. Robinson, however, was the last of the head gardeners to wield extensive power and influence. The era of the head gardener as king was over. It was killed off by the demise of the great estates, the agricultural depression of the 1880s, the importation of exotics such as pineapples, and by the growing habit among the wealthy of wintering on the Med, which led to the all-year garden being seen as a needless expense.

Leaves Alone

Robinson and Blomfield weren't alone in changing the appearance of gardens. New plants played their parts, too. Asiatic rhododendrons (many brought in by the plant hunter and Kew director Sir Joseph Hooker in the mid nineteenth century), bamboos and tree ferns could not fit into the neatly ordered ranks of Victorian bedding schemes any more than they could grace an Italianate terrace.

In Sussex and Cornwall, in particular, garden owners were funding plant hunters and placing the results in wooded valleys. Caerhays Castle in Cornwall provided a romantic valley setting for a host of introductions, including many rhododendrons, magnolias and camellias. Indeed, it was here that our glorious williamsii hybrid camellias first appeared, thanks to the owner of Caerhays, John Charles Williams, who crossed *C. japonica* with *C. saluenensis.* His descendants continue the family's plant-breeding tradition to the present day.

By the 1880s, new introductions were quick to find their way into smaller domestic gardens even when the owner could not afford to commission a plant hunter. As the nineteenth-century historian Alicia Amherst recounts:

Right: The romantic turret of Caerhays Castle, Cornwall, birthplace of a host of camellia hybrids and a fine collection of magnolias and rhododendrons.

Right and opposite:
Battersea Park's sub-tropical
gardens helped fan the craze
for leafy plants. Regular
features and pictures
appeared in the gardening
press of the 1860s.

22229   Battersea Park.
Sub-Tropical Gardens.

...hardy bamboos, Japanese maples and Iris began to arrive, but it was only during the last twenty years of the [nineteenth] century that they became cheap enough to be within the compass of small gardeners. The importation of them then began, 60,000 to 80,000 bulbs frequently arriving in one consignment.

Leafy specimens helped inspire the 1870s 'phyllomania', using plants that we would call architectural. Examples of the new planting styles could be seen in public parks, or if you didn't live in London, Liverpool or any other centre blessed with a park, you could read

about them, regularly and in some detail, in the burgeoning garden press. In the 1860s John Gibson, a plant hunter and former Chatsworth gardener, installed sub-tropical planting at Battersea Park, London. It was well publicized, and remained in vogue until the last decade of the century.

Contemporaries describe with awe the 'Bananas and Palms. India Rubber Plants and Indian Shoots [Cannas] in profusion, Coral plants, Dracaenas, Caladiums, and groups of handsome Tree ferns...'. These specimens thrived outside with the help of Gibson's

ingenious mounds made from broken brick covered with soil. This structure ensured that the roots could never become waterlogged and also helped to retain heat captured during the day. Gibson's lush, green jungle created a foil for Battersea's bedding.

Topiary

After the dazzling excesses of bedding out, topiary was seen as tasteful and traditional. It struck a chord with the Arts and Crafts' ethos of craftsmanship. William Morris carved a mythical Icelandic dragon, Fafnir, into a hedge at his garden at Kelmscot in

Oxfordshire. He, like many of the Arts and Crafts fraternity, enthused about topiary as an English tradition. The painter and poet Dante Gabriel Rossetti bought a thirty-year-old topiary armchair, and the fantastic garden of topiary shapes at Levens was much admired, along with a host of 'Olde English' topiary – much of it recently installed.

Topiary's most alluring and romantic incarnation was shrouded in secrecy for many years. The story of Elvaston Castle in Derbyshire reads like a fairy-tale. It was built in the first half of the nineteenth century by

Lord Harrington for his mistress. He created a series of magical gardens separated by hedges, some serpentine, and all clipped to velvety smoothness. There was an Alhambra; a garden of monkey puzzles; artificial lakes and rockwork; and a mass of extraordinary topiary, including peacocks, arbours, hedge windows, yew buttresses, domes, crowns and columns. Grafted trees included some that wept from a great height. Specimen trees were paraded in triple avenues. Few people knew about Elvaston because it was kept hidden from the world, a secret between a team of gardeners and their lovelorn and privacy-obsessed employers. But it was exceptional not only for its plant manipulation but also for its garden

rooms, so familiar in the twentieth century, that were made here for the first time since Tudor and Elizabethan times. The public finally got to see this wonderland, at a price, when the earl died in 1851.

Sporting Life

Elvaston's introverted atmosphere was a far cry from the busy, active life in most gardens by the end of the nineteenth century. The story behind John Singer Sargent's vast picture *Carnation Lily, Lily Rose* (1885), is instructive about a new attitude – sport had arrived in gardens and lived alongside an idealized image of gardens as wild, floriferous paradises. Sargent painted the picture in the Cotswold garden of one his friends, who grew lilies and carnations in pots to be arranged in an area of long grass as and when needed. The informal atmosphere, in which plants appeared to have naturalized in a meadow, caught the Robinsonian mood of the moment.

The light had to be perfect for the painting and, when it wasn't, Sargent would play tennis. Sport was becoming an important part of gardens. There was croquet (a game launched at the Great Exhibition and honed at Chastleton by Walter Jones Whitmore); archery; Spiropole; and lawn tennis – William Robinson added a court when he bought

Left and opposite: Sport
flourished in the garden,
and so did the Alpine craze.
This plant fashion reached
its zenith with this scale
model of the Matterhorn...in
the Thames valley.

The Dog's Grave

If sport added features to the garden, so too did the vogue for alpine plants. In the early twentieth century Sir Frank Crisp made a scale model of the Matterhorn, complete with tin chamois, to show off the alpine plants at his large garden, Friar Park, near Henley-on-Thames. Underneath the Matterhorn's peak he built caves and pools filled with tricks and illusions that were illuminated by a new-fangled thing called electricity. His garden became a thinking man's version of a Disney theme park. But his lavish rockwork made rival gardeners jealous and culminated in a thinly veiled attack on the baronet by the plant hunter and 'Father of English Rock Gardening' Reginald Farrer. This in turn provoked Ellen Willmott, the renowned plantswoman, to picket the contemporary equivalent of the Chelsea Flower Show with rude leaflets. The feud caused uproar.

Gravetye Manor. Shuttlecocks, balls and arrows were now whirled about the garden with such enthusiasm that they created a thriving market for 'Bayliss's Ornamental Game-proof Hurdles' (they look like iron fences that can be seen in some parks today), to give some protection to the planting.

Sporting enthusiasm extended to public parks, too. In Battersea Park around the turn of the century a bowling green, grass tennis courts, three gymnasia and a boat house were installed. Photographs taken as early as 1895 show women riding bicycles.

Lesser-known suburban echoes of the Alps were mocked by the gardening press as 'The Dog's Grave', 'Almond Pudding' and 'Devil's Lapful'. The mournful heaps were made from old crockery, fossils, pieces of church window, bricks, flints and chunks of glass; and sometimes they were painted 'Brunswick Green' or daubed with various colours in the vain hope of making the debris look more like

Above: Plant hunter Reginald Farrer's rock garden in Clapham, Lancashire. This was a serious affair, although not as spectacular as Sir Frank Crisp's, which might explain Farrer's attack on the baronet.

a pile of natural rocks. The paint may have been new but the rockwork urge was not. In the eighteenth century it had appeared as grottos, and in the early nineteenth century it ranged from tiny mock ruins and grottos to Henry Trevor's vast quarry garden at The Plantation in Norwich, which included a Gothic steeple as a fountain centrepiece. Now, though, rockwork enthusiasm was fuelled by alpine flowers, by Robinson's book *Alpine Flowers for English Gardens* and by Reginald Farrer's plant-hunting expeditions. These visual graveyards made a vivid contrast to the exquisite plants they were designed to display.

As if the aesthetic qualities of most rock gardens were not dubious enough, they also attracted the first garden gnomes to Britain. Sir Charles Isham imported the creatures from

Germany to his grounds at Lamport Hall, Northampton, in about 1860.

Cornucopia

Reginald Farrer not only popularized alpine plants but also introduced a host of garden plants that are now familiar in our gardens, such as the weeping *Buddleia alternifolia*. And his books conjure up vivid pictures of the places he explored. This is how he put it in *The Rainbow Bridge*:

I am...spinning a rainbow bridge, far-flung over black depths, towards the golden unrecoverable past... Those...that think that this rainbow bridge of mine will carry them also out of a storm, back into a forgotten country of calm, are very welcome, indeed, to make the journey...with me...

He loathed the hardships he had to endure in his quest, but when he found a 'new' plant:

...there stared at me a new Gentian, a Gentian that instantly obliterates all others of its race ... And its beauty! ...I stood rapt in contemplation before the actual plant, the last and the greatest event of my second season, and well worth the whole two years' expedition anyhow, merely to have seen it.

On the same expedition his Chinese quilted dressing-gown caught fire while he was warming himself against a brazier. It did him no lasting harm but, like many plant hunters, he suffered for his work. In 1920 Farrer died in Upper Burma, aged forty.

In a sense he was a victim of Britain's burgeoning empire. In the second half of the century Britain doubled the area of the globe under its control: imperial pink covered the whole of Australia, New Zealand, India and Canada, as well as parts of the Far East, Africa and South America, although the acquisitions looked more impressive on paper than they were in economic reality. Whatever the bold economic results of the increased empire, it continued to be used as a treasure box by plant hunters. Some pioneers forged into unknown and hostile territories, and most had

to live on their wits at one time or another. Frank Kingdon Ward, of Meconopsis 'Blue Poppy' fame, used opium as a currency; George Forrest died on the job, having witnessed mass executions, and Ernest 'Chinese' Wilson narrowly escaped arrest as a spy. Luckily for us, he was spared and introduced three thousand plants, one thousand of which are familiar today.

One of my favourites is the regal lily, which nearly cost Wilson a leg. He was working in Asia at around the same time as Farrer and found the gorgeous scented plant in one of China's wilder areas in 1905. It was love at first sight, as Wilson's description shows:

High up on the mountainside...this lily...greets the weary traveller...in thousands, aye, in tens

Above: The exquisite blue of gentians like this have captured the hearts of plant lovers for years.

of thousands. Its slender stems, each 2–4 feet tall...are crowned...with several large funnel-shaped flowers more or less wine coloured without, pure white and lustrous within the tube and each stamen tipped with a golden anther.

For some reason the plant didn't catch on, but Wilson, who was determined that it should be appreciated by a wider audience, made the harrowing 2,000-mile trip back across China to the borders of Tibet to collect it in greater numbers (a crazy mission given the plant's astonishing ability to multiply). It was 1910 and his fourth trip to China, and yet even 'Chinese' Wilson loathed the area where he found the regal lily: 'no more barren and repelling country can be imagined,' he wrote. As his party made its way back to Shanghai, a landslide crashed down a mountainside and smashed Wilson's leg. It became infected and nearly had to be amputated, leaving him with his 'lily limp' for the rest of his life.

Some of Wilson's introductions had speedy successes. He found the yellow *Meconopsis integrifolia* in 1903. The following spring it was displayed at Chelsea's forerunner, the 'Temple Show', and the seeds were distributed in September.

Above: The Japanese-British Exhibition at White City in 1910.

Orchids continued to be prized by rich garden owners, who commissioned plant hunters to find new specimens. The Rothschilds devoted glasshouses to the plant, and the colonial secretary Joseph Chamberlain, who was rarely without an orchid in his buttonhole, ran 13 glasshouses in his Birmingham gardens.

Japan in Fashion

Farrer is usually associated with alpine plants, but in 1903 he lived in Tokyo and wrote about Japanese gardens in *The Gardens of Asia*. It accelerated the craze for 'Japanese' gardens, which began in the 1860s with increased trade between Japan and the outside world.

Right: Jane Loudon
pioneered gardening for
middle class women with
practical advice by the
barrowload; including a
detailed essay on digging
for 'small and delicately
formed hands and feet'.

Mrs. LOUDON's

GARDENING

FOR

LADIES.

LONDON:
JOHN MURRAY, ALBEMARLE STREET.
1843.

The great plantsman E. A. Bowles, who created
a 'Lunatic Asylum' of plant oddities at Enfield,
confirmed the craze when he made his own
'Japanese' garden in the early twentieth
century:

...before it had got far that sort of thing
became fashionable, and bronze cranes and
stone lanterns met one in all sorts of

unsuitable surroundings, the Temple Show
began to bristle with giant toads, and pagodas,
and jingling glass bird-scarers frightened the
last idea of reproducing a page of Condor right
out of my head.

The usual configuration involved a Shinto
shrine; a stone lantern washed with rice water
to encourage moss growth; Korean pines,
azaleas and spiraeas, and a curved wooden
bridge crossing a pool of water. Puccini's
Madame Butterfly had a lot to answer for.
So did Batsford Park in Gloucestershire, with
its wealth of Japanese trees and bamboos.

London's 1862 International Exhibition
included a Japanese court and, in the
following decade, a miniature Japanese village
appeared in London's Alexandra Palace. It was
laid out by a Japanese landscaper. There was
a little mound, a bridge and 'a stream with
which we are familiar on the Chinese plates
and dishes – we seem only to want the
Weeping Willow to make it complete'. That
contemporary report, happily mixing Chinese
with Japanese, was typical. Nobody worried
about mingling oriental traditions. It was
foreign, after all. In 1910 London's Japanese–
British Exhibition struck a more authentic
note with a full-size, double-storey tea-house
and bridge.

Japan appeared at Cliveden in Buckinghamshire, Heale House in Wiltshire, Cowden in Scotland and Tatton Park in Cheshire (the last two both made by Japanese gardeners); and at Easton Lodge in Essex, where the Prince of Wales's mistress, Daisy, had a Japanese area added. Japanese garden ideas even appeared inside houses, thanks to William Robinson, who recommended placing branches of sloe, plum and crab to break buds indoors: 'The Japanese have taught us to see the beauty of form and line in a single twig or branch,' he wrote in *The English Flower Garden*.

Lady Gardeners

Robinson's great friend Gertrude Jekyll would help create one of the most enduring garden styles in history, as we shall see in the next chapter. Yet she grew up at a time when corsets were so tight that they could make a woman faint, and skirts picked up muck or moisture with every step. This was the lot of the increasing number of late nineteenth-century lady gardeners, who were quite different from the poor, itinerant weeding women recorded since the eighteenth century. Lady gardeners discussed the difficulty of working in unsuitable clothes – but did little about it other than explaining how to avoid sun-burned wrists, as the following mid

nineteenth-century columnist describes:

There is no doubt that a lady's dress is not one very well suited for gardening; all we can do is to obviate its disadvantages ... actual work in the garden does not improve its appearance. A large apron, and gloves are some protection; but what I have found better is a dark shirt. Gloves are indispensable to prevent the earth getting in at the wrist. I have seen ladies make gauntlets of strong unbleached linen fastened to the glove; this is quite as effectual for protecting the dress and for preventing that sun-burning of the wrist which is the frequent fate of lady gardeners ...

1897
"THE GENTLEWOMAN"
CALENDAR for
October

" "The Gentlewoman" is the Ideal Ladies' Paper "

Above: By the end of the nineteenth century gardening had become a fashionable hobby for ladies.

Right: This type of
conservatory window was
an ideal gardening venue
for less robust – or less
enthusiastic – Victorian
lady gardeners.

Jane Loudon recommended Ladies Gardening Gauntlets in her groundbreaking book *Gardening for Ladies*, which was published in 1840. It was popular and influential both in Britain and in the USA. With her usual diplomatic deference to husbands, she explained that gardening was a perfectly respectable activity for ladies. In doing so, she paved the way for the rise of the lady gardener, who was to colour and shape the twentieth-century garden.

By the end of the nineteenth century women were, increasingly, working in gardens and writing about them. Alicia Amherst's *History of Gardening in England* (1895) forms the (unacknowledged) basis for some twentieth-century garden histories; Mrs Haweis took a more practical approach; and Gertrude Jekyll was beginning her gentle garden revolution.

Amherst maintained that she had learnt the practical side of gardening from her mother, who was devoted to the subject 'long years before it was considered a fashionable pastime for ladies'. Mrs Haweis confirmed the vogue for lady's gardening activities in her book *Rus in Urbe or Flowers That Thrive in London Gardens & Smoky Towns*, which cost a shilling and probably appeared in 1886.

The frontispiece showed two children playing beside a stream with a basket and various flowers, but the theme of the redoubtable Mrs Haweis is strictly London. She explained that the city still had its fair share of excellent gardens, particularly in Bayswater, Chelsea and St John's Wood, where specimen trees and orchards abounded. She listed the plants that could brave city pollution, extolled the health-giving properties of plants and gave her formula for a low-cost, instant garden:

The first thing to do is to remove entirely the dank, sour, exhausted soil which clogs the beds

in many neglected London gardens. Ten shillings will go a long way towards this. Good rich loam and manure can be ordered through any respectable florist or store, and a shilling's worth of seeds, with a barrowful of gravel, will make a decent scene of a dirty little wilderness. Tile edging is cheap. A small fountain with a pipe laid on a top cistern costs little. Rockeries are easily got up. Turf itself can be persuaded.

Conservatories had her seal of approval as a 'charming outlet at all times' and in summer 'an airy tea room'. In a similarly twenty-first-century mode, she attacked cats as possessing 'no homes, no principles, nor remorse'. Her solution was a cat tax.

Ladies with a less robust constitution could make do with a conservatory window – a

structure in the style of a Wardian case built on to the outside wall of a villa. There is one at 18 Stafford Terrace, just off Kensington High Street in London.

In 1908 Frances Wolseley published *Gardening for Women*. Then, like snowdrops in spring, horticultural colleges for women appeared: at Glynde, Waterperry, Reading University, Studley and Swanley. The RHS was more reticent. Its roller-coaster fortunes had improved thanks to Sir Thomas Hanbury's gift, in 1903, of 24 hectares of garden at Wisley in Surrey. The following year the society moved to its current HQ in Vincent Square, London. But women were not to play a central part in the society for some time. It gave grants to some of the women's gardening schools but only reluctantly allowed female

Above: Irises at the RHS gardens at Wisley, Surrey, in 1897.

students at Wisley during the Second World War when Swanley was bombed – and then only on condition that they found accommodation elsewhere. It took until 1946 for the society to appoint its first woman professional to the staff.

Half a century earlier the prospect of professional lady gardeners was greeted with boos and hisses from the male-dominated media. Swanley's inception attracted the following press comment: '...is the 12s a week for the twelve hours day really a fitting reward to the delicately nurtured girl for three years study and £140 spent on college fees?' Similarly discouraging comments were made in *St James' Gazette*:

The managers of Kew Gardens have recently decided to admit women among their gardeners...the wages are 10s a week; the ladies must wear rational dress – not a particularly cheap thing to provide; and the hours are six to six in summer, with lectures to be attended afterwards. When these are over the weary 'gardeneress' has...to continue studies, rest her back and ponder over the problem of life on £26 a year.

Ditties were made up about Kew's latest recruits, and visitors would come to the garden in the hope of seeing the poor creatures kitted out in their 'uniform': vast and unattractive blue serge suits (bloomer-like trousers and waistcoats) and grey flannel shirts with tweed caps.

Looking back, it seems miraculous that the professional female gardener ever ventured out of the potting-shed.

Below: Privileged children
played gardens with
miniature tools. Others had
to work long hours using
full-sized equipment.

A Children's Garden

Like women, children were expected to know
their place – which meant mostly being out of
the way. At the end of the nineteenth century,
however, they began to acquire some kind
of official recognition in the garden after
magazine reports about children's gardens
at Osborne House on the Isle of Wight. The
gardens had been created for Queen Victoria
and Prince Albert's children earlier in the
century. *The Gardener's Chronicle* was allowed
to visit in 1897 and reported:

The Swiss chalet...is surrounded by the flower
beds and small kitchen gardens that used to
belong to the young princes and princesses ...
The little garden tools are still preserved there,
including the wheel barrow which was once
part of the Prince of Wales's equipment, and
bears the letters 'P. W.' upon it. The initials ...
of most of the Royal children may still be seen
on the handles of one or other of these very
interesting relics of the time when the Queen's
children were as young as her great
grandchildren are now.

Prince Albert used to buy the vegetables his
children grew and send them to the royal
kitchens.

The Royal example made a children's garden

highly desirable in fashionable households.
Manufacturers latched on to the craze and
produced miniature tools, including boxed
sets for dressing show chrysanthemums.

For the less practically minded child there
was always Alice and her various adventures,
many of which had garden or plant themes.
In her 'Adventure with the Live Flowers' she
interrogates a rose bush:

'Aren't you sometimes frightened at being
planted out here with nobody to take care of
you?'
'There's that tree in the middle,' said the Rose.
'But what could it do if danger came?'
Alice asked.
'It could bark,' said the Rose.

4 Arts and Crafts Fulfilled

Perfect Early Twentieth-century Compromise

Opposite: The Arts and Crafts-style garden dominated the twentieth century. Gertrude Jekyll's home, Munstead Wood, was a supreme example.

The guerrilla war of words between Blomfield and Robinson was a legacy of a centuries-old conundrum: how much should Nature (or at least man's version of Nature) be allowed in a man-made setting which is by definition unnatural? At the turn of the century a new style came up with the answer. It melded structure with planting, and, to date, no one has come up with a more popular compromise between flowers and formality than the gardens created by Gertrude Jekyll and Edwin Lutyens.

THE ALPINE GARDEN SOCIETY

1906
Jekyll and Lutyens's first major collaboration, at Hestercombe

1910
Lawrence Johnston starts work on Hidcote garden. The property was bought three years earlier by his mother

1913
The Chelsea Flower Show begins

1914–18
First World War
Marie Stopes's bestseller *Married Love* published

1920
Heather Muir begins the garden at Kiftsgate
Chatsworth's Great Stove blown up

1922
BBC radio begins

1928
Birds Eye sells its first packaged frozen foods

1929
Institute of Landscape Architects formed
Alpine Society founded

1930s
Hitler bans psychoanalysis. Freud escapes to live in Hampstead. Arnold Schoenberg exiled by the Nazis and settles in the USA

1930
Vita Sackville-West and Harold Nicolson buy Sissinghurst Castle

1933
Phyllis Reiss begins Tintinhull

DIG FOR VICTORY LEAFLET
NUMBER 20   (NEW SERIES)
ISSUED BY THE MINISTRY OF AGRICULTURE

Opposite: Jekyll and Lutyens's collaboration at Hestercombe, Somerset, in 1906. The garden's rotunda created a grand entrance to the sunken gardens of rills, pergolas and glorious planting.

They were a most unlikely couple. Jekyll was a prim, middle-aged artist/plantswoman, Lutyens a young, skittish architect, but together they perfected the Arts and Crafts garden and made it Britain's most enduring style. Their graceful combination of flowers and formality solved the power struggle between horticulturalists and architects with a garden style that continues to flourish on both sides of the Atlantic.

Jekyll was born in 1843, the year that John Loudon died. She trained as an artist and knew some of the Impressionists but, as her eyesight deteriorated, she turned to gardening and designed her mother's garden at Munstead Wood in Surrey. In 1889 she met Lutyens at a tea party in Surrey when she was 45 and he was 20. As Jekyll left, having said nothing to him during tea, she invited Lutyens to Munstead Wood. They went on to form one of the most influential partnerships in garden history, in which he planned the hard landscaping and she the planting. Sometimes he built the house, too, so integrating house and garden harmoniously. Jekyll and Lutyens made about 112 gardens and their style was and is still copied assiduously.

The gardens captured the dying moments of a leisured middle-class life propped up by

battalions of staff inside and outside the house. Rustic furniture, back in fashion after nearly a century, added to the restful, rural feel, although some items were sophisticated constructions. Stained-glass panels decorated doors, and ornate thatched structures posed as 'rustic lawn tennis houses', summer-houses or sports houses.

By the First World War Jekyll and Lutyens's gardens were the height of fashion. The classic style rarely looks out of place even in the early twenty-first century. In fact, the vocabulary of a Jekyll/Lutyens garden is as familiar now as it was in the early twentieth century. The main framework around the house is made from rustically dressed stone, hand-made brick, wood, clipped box and yew. This is softened by voluptuous, colour-coordinated borders of perennials and bulbs. Water lilies bloom in a square, sunken lily pool. Semicircular alcove pools in retaining walls stand at the head of rills (narrow formal streams) or long, thin iris-filled canals. Fans of semicircular stone steps make every change of level aesthetically pleasing. Pergolas, based on old English designs (rather than Renaissance models favoured by nineteenth-century formalists), support roses, clematis, honeysuckle and other scented climbers. At Jekyll and Lutyens's Hestercombe garden in Somerset, a Russian

Right: Hemispherical pools at the head of rills, like this one at Hestercombe, with stone whirlpools became one of Lutyens's signature features.

vine clambered around the original vast pergola. Cracks between stone-paved paths are speckled with herbs, and towards the perimeter of the garden the hard landscaping gives way to larger, less regimented plantings linking the garden to the landscape beyond. In these transitionary areas the plants include Japanese knotweed and giant hogweed, first popularized by Robinson (and now the cause of major problems: the knotweed is destabilizing motorways and the hogweed causes skin burns).

Many of the plants that Jekyll used – Madonna lilies, delphinium, iris, purple gladioli, hollyhocks, snapdragons, pinks, valerian, globe thistles, rabbits ears, santolina, nepeta, elephants' ears and lavender – are still commonplace. Others have vanished along with an era when most nurseries carried a sensational number of plant varieties – two and a half thousand was not uncommon. Jekyll's own nursery was typical of the time. The wars destroyed this cornucopia and, even at the start of the Second World War, 'good' nurseries could muster barely a thousand varieties.

The origins of Jekyll and Lutyens's garden style can be traced back to William Morris and the rest of the Arts and Crafts movement, as well as to propagandists for 'wild' herbaceous gardens, such as Robert Marnock and William Robinson. Jekyll briefly edited Robinson's journal, *The Garden*, before it became part of *Homes and Gardens*. William Wildsmith is another who should be credited. His work at Heckfield Place in Hampshire, trumpeted in his extensive journalism, showed how to plant formal beds with an abundance of unstaked flowers such as dahlias, nasturtiums, heliotropes and marguerites. He also popularized light grey and whitish-green in colour schemes – a precursor of the grey-foliage plants used in so many of Jekyll's schemes.

Spectrum Theory

Colour in the garden had zipped in and out of fashion during the nineteenth century. By the last decades of the century, lush green plantings had tempered bright bedding schemes, and succulents had introduced a new and relatively restful form of bedding. Jekyll brought back colour in an entirely different form. Like mid nineteenth-century colour theorists, she was interested in colour relationships, and she developed her own colour principles based on Turner's painting and Michel Chevreul's book *The Principles of Harmony and Contrast of Colours and Their Application to the Art*s (1854). Chevreul's colour

Opposite: Madonna lilies were among Jekyll's most favoured plants. Some still flourish in the spot where she planted them around a century ago.

Cool blues and whites at either end and a
climax of hot reds and oranges at the centre.
Ideally, this was set off by a backdrop of a yew
hedge or stone wall. Her planting plans were
precise and provided colour for many months
of the year.

The Cost of War

Many Jekyll and Lutyens gardens were
installed by the onset of the First World War,
which dealt a fatal blow to the nineteenth
century's great, extravagant gardens. A
generation of young men died in the trenches.
The story of Heligan's gardeners, wiped out by
the war, is well known thanks to the 1990s
renovation of the Cornish estate, but there
were many more casualties, human and
otherwise. In 1920 the Duke of Devonshire
had Chatsworth's Great Stove blown up, and a
host of lesser-known hothouses were simply
abandoned. Of the opulent gardens that had
managed to survive the First World War,
many were killed off by the Second, including
the Countess of Warwick's Easton Lodge and
Miriam Rothschild's garden near
Peterborough, where she allowed nature to
overwhelm her father's Edwardian Italianate
garden and the glasshouses that once supplied
prize orchids to RHS shows. Nesfield's garden,
in front of Kew's palm house, was put down to
onions, and much of the rest of that historic

theories, popularized in this country from the
1840s, influenced bedding-out aficionados, the
Arts and Crafts movement, as well as artists
from Pissarro to Cézanne, and leading
Victorian gardeners. His colour wheel, still
in use today in one form or another, has the
primary colours spaced out evenly around the
perimeter of the wheel, with all the shades
arranged in order between them.

Jekyll's signature planting scheme applied this
spectrum principle to her borders, putting

landscape went over to root vegetables. Even the dazzling rhododendrons and azaleas collected and bred by Lionel de Rothschild at Exbury were left to their own devices in the 1940s when the house was turned over to war use.

Everyone, including the Royal Family, was supposed to make their garden productive. Photographs taken in 1917 show Queen Mary, in a large hat, and George V, in braces, digging potatoes at Windsor. The implausible scene reflected the deep concern about wartime food production. Similarly, during the Second World War, Royal Lodge gardens were ploughed up for food production – one

photograph shows the future Queen Elizabeth, with a spade on her shoulder, and Princess Margaret, with a corgi in her wooden barrow, 'working' in the gardens.

Public and royal parks, from Kensington Gardens and the land around the Albert Memorial to obscure local parks, were turned over to food production, and in 1917 display gardens showing how to grow vegetables were made at Battersea Park.

The need for home-grown food during both wars destroyed many ornamental gardens and invigorated the allotment movement, as well as local production forces, such as the Spade

Above: Edward VII's mistress 'Darling Daisy', Countess of Warwick, created Easton Lodge garden in Essex with the help of Harold Peto.

Opposite: The future Queen
Elizabeth II and her sister,
Princess Margaret, were in
a long tradition of Royal
gardening...although their
tools and shoes look
remarkably clean.

Clubs in the north. In 1919 the RHS sent seeds and tools to aid post-war France. And the society issued wall charts on the control of pests and disease to help 'the allotment movement, which, during the war, has spread so happily from one end of the country to the other'.

The aftermath of each war caused a flutter of editorial comment about the difficulty of finding gardeners and the need to reduce maintenance levels. Time-saving devices were a favoured solution, and one writer enthusiastically referred to an early American method of automatic irrigation: '[this] economic system of pipes combined with the use of automatic sprinklers will obviate hours of work'. Two 1925 handbooks, both published by *Country Life*, were aimed at the garden owner working solo or at least with minimal help. Times had indeed changed, as an advertisement for the books recognized: 'When one's gardening hours are limited and the need for activity is urgent the ponderous volume which deals exhaustively with every phase and aspect of its subject cannot be simply read.'

Problems faced by garden owners in the 1920s were summed up by one journal as follows: '... before the war, many gardens were run on

extravagant lines, but then labour and coal – always the most expensive part of the garden – were cheaper than in these post-war days.' Extravagant was the right description. At the Rothschilds' colourful and productive garden, Gunnersbury, hot water was added to outdoor pools to bring on the water lilies. And, when Edward VII came to stay, orchids were added to every lady's table setting.

Gardens were going to have to change. They did – along with the people who ran them. Garden owners, women included, had to take on an increasing amount of the donkey-work. As a result, women's gardening clothes became more practical – although Jekyll appears to have been slightly ahead of her time. After their first meeting, Lutyens described Jekyll as wearing 'a short blue skirt that in no way hid her ankles'. By the late 1920s, ladies' made-to-measure 'gardening breeches and jodhpurs' were advertised in many of the gardening journals.

During the Second World War enterprising companies were using the conflict to sell their goods. This 1940 *Amateur Gardening* advertisement is typical: 'By producing home-grown vegetables you are giving invaluable help to our shipping by using Clays fertilizer – Just the feed vegetables need.' In the same year

Opposite: Growing your own food was an important part of the war effort and inspired great creativity, as this air raid shelter garden shows.

the Ministry of Agriculture took out a whole page of a popular gardening journal to show a picture of a foot on a spade, and the slogan: 'Step on it! Dig now, don't delay – get your own garden ready to grow vegetables – especially the kinds you can store. Apply to your local council for an allotment and dig with all your might. Vegetables will be scarcer. Victory may well be won by the country with the most food. It is up to every man and woman to step on it now and make every garden a VICTORY GARDEN. DIG for VICTORY NOW!'

People dug like crazy and then, after each war, threw in their trowels. In 1900 half a million allotments were in use; the figure rose to one and a half million during the First World War, slumped in the post-war years and then climbed back again to one and a half million during the Second World War, only to decline again in the 1950s. By 1964, fewer than 730,000 people were working allotments.

Variations on a Theme

Middle-class gardens soldiered on through the two wars without huge changes in style. Those who wanted to do something unusual with their gardens had few examples to follow. Christopher Tunnard tried to enthuse the British with ideas about the 'modern'

garden but, as we shall see in the following chapter, these sparks of influence would take a while to ignite. Then there were the eccentric one-offs, such as Lord Berners' garden at Faringdon in Oxfordshire, with its doves dyed green, purple and red, its monkey puzzle alley, outdoor chandeliers and, later, fake flowers. It acquired a certain celebrity when Nancy Mitford used Berners, and his home, as the model for Lord Merlin in *The Pursuit of Love* (1945). Mainstream gardens were essentially variations on the Arts and Crafts theme. There were Harold Peto's large gardens, including his own at Iford Manor, Wiltshire; Vita Sackville-West and Harold Nicolson's Sissinghurst in Kent; Lawrence Johnston's Hidcote in Gloucestershire; and Phyllis Reiss's Tintinhull in Somerset. The gardens were the outdoor equivalent of a well-made chintz armchair, with all the comfortable English charm that implies.

The 'garden room' idea was revived and given new meaning by Johnston and then Sackville-West, who created distinct atmospheres in each 'room'. At Hidcote the red borders rather than hard landscaping gave a bold statement in planting, as did Sackville-West's renowned White Garden. Like Sissinghurst, Tintinhull followed Hidcote's garden room example. Over the road from Hidcote, Heather Muir began the planterly garden of Kiftsgate in Gloucestershire in 1920. The eponymous rose, *Rosa filipes* 'Kiftsgate', still dominates one area.

This garden era was spearheaded by women, often in partnership with men: Jekyll and Lutyens; Sackville-West and Nicolson; and Reiss and her husband the Captain. Norah Lindsay, who mixed her plant brio with a passion for Italian features at Sutton Courtenay in Oxfordshire, gardened with Lawrence Johnston in later life. All of them owned their gardens, and many wrote about and publicized their innovations and designs, just as the head gardeners had done for so much of the nineteenth century.

One of the few public gardens to be made in the first half of the twentieth century was the Savill Garden in Berkshire, which began life when a ranger planted an area of Windsor Great Park. The ranger, Eric Savill, persuaded friends, parks gardeners in London and anyone else who would listen to give him rhododendrons, azaleas, lilies, camellias, magnolias and bog-loving gunnera, primulas, ferns and rheums for the acid valley he had chosen for his project. He planted informally in a style similar to many turn-of-the-century woodland gardens, such as Caerhays, Leonardslee and High Beeches.

Down the road at Royal Lodge the Duke and Duchess of York (the future King George VI and Queen Elizabeth) heard about Savill's project and lent their support. They were keen gardeners and had helped clear their own garden at Royal Lodge before asking two great British designers, Russell Page and Geoffrey Jellicoe, to install a terrace and help with the planting. Later the royal couple followed Savill's example and planted swathes of azaleas and rhododendrons in their thirty acres. The future Queen was fond of scented flowers, so roses and woodland lilies were worked into Royal Lodge gardens, along with plants such as *Magnolia stellata*, which was to become popular in many small front gardens.

London gardeners could find inspiration in, or rather on, department stores. The 1938 Derry & Toms roof garden in Kensington, Ralph Hancock's 1.5-acre creation, was a glamorous finale to any shopping expedition, as my great-aunt Carys used to note. Pools, streams, palms and flamingos made the gardens seem otherworldly. Roughly 5,000 plant varieties grew on 30 in of topsoil. In design terms the garden was – and remains – a curious mix: a Moorish courtyard with touches of the Generalife in Granada, an English woodland, and a Tudor area. In this it was a typical of the disparate styles that continued to crowd into gardens.

Down the road in Knightsbridge, at that other great department store, Harrods, well-heeled shoppers had another treat. In 1911 Harrods Rock Tea Gardens appeared. 'Amid scenes of rural splendour, fresh-flowering plants, rustic bridges and waterfalls the London visitor will find this an ideal place for afternoon tea', was how one picture postcard caption described the scene, although 'rural splendour' was hardly accurate. However, those inspired by the rural splendour could buy the Harrods version, inside the store, where one of the great halls was decked out with massive displays of trees and plants, all of them for sale.

Size Matters

Londoners, and other city dwellers, have always gardened in small spaces. Abundant window-boxes and minute backyards are recorded in the eighteenth and nineteenth centuries and, by 1919, the London Gardens Guild had branches in most boroughs. Like the florists' societies of the eighteenth and nineteenth centuries, the guild encouraged gardening in small spaces.

After the First World War, however, even relatively prosperous suburban and country families had accepted the smaller garden as a fact of life. Not that size hindered the installation of 'essential' features. In 1927 the *Daily Mail*'s Home Exhibition displayed a 120 ft garden that included a tennis court, a vegetable area and a washing line.

The shrinking middle-class garden was gradually acknowledged by garden writers such as Vita Sackville-West, Sissinghurst's creator. She wrote in her *Observer* column about a 'very small' garden, although her notion of 'small' is interesting. 'From time to time I get letters from owners of very small gardens,' she began, then quoted a typical letter:

Our plot is the usual commonplace rectangle, 45ft by 175ft, but I am resolved NOT to have a commonplace garden. Our house stands 40ft back from the road, with this pocket-handkerchief frontage... We hope to plant a camomile lawn, and I have ideas about a lavender hedge...and we want one or two trees, NOT the usual commonplace cherry...

Sackville-West replies that if she had to move into a bungalow, housing estate, or council house (the mind boggles), 'I should have no hesitation at all about ruffling the front garden into a wildly unsymmetrical mess and making it as near as possible into a cottage garden.'

That 'unsymmetrical mess' would not have been popular with the growing mass of tiny garden owners. Idealized pictures of late 1940s' gardens, the type used by advertisers in the popular gardening press, show a neatly striped, rectangular lawn with a round bed of conifers at the centre, surrounded by a crazy paving path with a neat mixed bed between the path and the wooden fence.

Garden Cities and New Towns

This idealized advertisers' garden was not appropriate to the 'new towns' that were being built for the expanding population.

The philosophy of the new conglomerations was forged in Ebenezer Howard's book *Garden Cities of Tomorrow*, which suggested a cap of 32,000 on town population, a garden for each house and a green belt around the lot. This began to be made reality in 1903, when Barry Parker and Raymond Unwin began building the first 'garden city' at Letchworth. The point was to give a greater number of people a better standard of living – an idea generated by nineteenth-century philanthropists, including Jeremy Bentham, Robert Owen and the Cadbury brothers. The first garden cities and their precursors, such as Bedford Park, which was built in the 1870s, were well served by versions of the Arts and Crafts garden.

The new, post-Second World War generation of new towns, which were based on garden city principles, reflected the simpler lines of modern and Scandinavian architecture. Some

front gardens were made without boundaries, and all of them needed a new style of garden. It was a while before a fittingly radical garden style evolved to suit these new outdoor spaces, but the government tried to do its bit, and in 1948 the Ministry of Health produced a one-shilling pamphlet called *Our Garden*. It included plenty of black and white pictures of suburban and urban gardens, and a two-page headline aimed to overcome contemporary prejudice: 'Many towns are beautiful. New Towns can be lovely too.' The suggestions were plodding – shrubs and other relatively low-maintenance plants to soften the brave new buildings – but at least they raised the question of what type of garden the new towns needed.

By 1958 Dame Sylvia Crowe, who helped formulate the government's 1940s' White Paper on new towns, had moved on: 'One of the weaknesses of the garden city style of layout is the even, overall distribution of the open spaces among the buildings, so that no view is either wholly closed or wholly open.' She was also sorely aware of the need to create higher-density housing to cater for the increasing population. Her suggested solution was shared gardens – as in communal gardens – and linked park systems, like that in Boston to provide 'those simple pleasures of life

which the countryman has always enjoyed'. This was exactly Ebenezer Howard's ambition for garden cities half a century earlier.

Chelsea Flowers

Country pleasures were an over-ambitious aim for those living in 'old' cities such as London – but at least they had parks and flower shows. In the early years of the century the RHS began what is now the most famous flower show in the world. The Horticultural Society's regular meetings, where papers were read and plants exhibited, developed into its first show in 1827. In 1862 the society began the Great Spring Show and moved from its first site, in Kensington, to the Temple Gardens on the embankment. Then, in 1913, it went to the grounds of the Royal Hospital, Chelsea. The Chelsea Flower Show had been born. From the beginning, Chelsea displayed the cream of national and international horticulture, fashions and oddities.

To many, Jekyll included, the RHS – and the Chelsea show – were the backbone of British gardens. As Jekyll wrote:

...the fortnightly meetings of the Royal Horticultural Society, and their most important one in the early summer [i.e. Chelsea]...are of the utmost value... The love

of gardening has so greatly grown and spread within the last few years, that the need of really good and beautiful garden flowers is already far in advance of the demand of so-called 'florist's flowers'.

In 1920 the RHS made an attempt to spread its services beyond the south-east by holding a show at Cardiff. Other provincial centres had been used for shows in the late nineteenth century for the same reason. But the bad weather made the show a wash-out. The reporter from *The Garden* tried to put a cheery perspective on it by boarding a raft *inside* the exhibition tent to inspect the displays, which included an 'exquisite collection of hippeastrums'. After that it was hardly surprising that the RHS retreated to the warmth and safety of shows at Westminster and Chelsea.

On top of the shows and meetings, the society was continuing its scientific work.

The term 'genetics', a 1990s' buzzword, was coined in 1906 by Cambridge professor of biology, William Bateson, at an RHS conference. The same man was responsible, this time while reading on his way to an RHS lecture, for rediscovering Gregor Mendel's 1865 work on hybridization.

The society was thriving. Membership rose to 25,000 in 1928, more than three times its size at the beginning of the century. It was spreading its wings and becoming increasingly involved in the design and history of gardens as well as their horticulture. Meanwhile, science had been forging ahead.

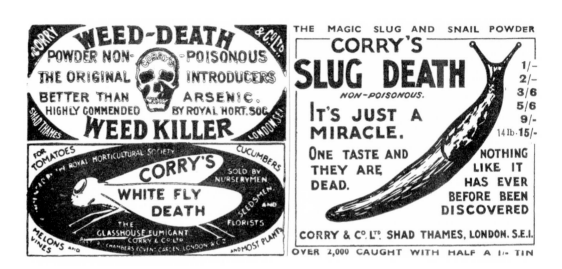

Radio Active

Dangerous chemicals were still commonplace throughout the garden world, as well as in agriculture – the first crop-dusting plane took off in 1921 in Ohio. The attitude to chemicals is best summed up by an advertisement for a liquid fertilizer. It shows a picture of a horse and cart of manure with a large cross superimposed and a caption that reads: 'WHY BOTHER? Liquinure is BETTER...the perfectly balanced plant food...'

Frederick Keeble's 1939 book *Science Lends a Hand in the Garden* was typical of the confident and relaxed attitude to chemicals. It was an accepted practice to use sulphuric acid to eradicate potato blight, and to spray fruit with a range of toxins. The book, a collection of

avuncular articles from *Gardeners' Chronicle*, put chemicals at the centre of the gardener's armoury, but it also encouraged composting, caring for the soil and good husbandry.

...what a lot of trouble it saves the gardener to know, as Science tells him [heaven forbid the gardener should be female], that Celery leaf spot comes with the seed, and the grub of Celery leaf fly comes out of the soil. Knowing this, he makes his seedsmen give him clean seed and he sows his celery plants in sterilized, or at all events fresh, soil and keeps them in frames or greenhouses till they are ready to harden off...

Cyanide was used to kill off scale insects on citrus, peach, apple and other fruit. A tent was erected over each tree, then sulphuric acid was poured on to potassium cyanide and – hey presto – noxious fumes billowed out, killing everything in sight.

Arsenate of lead paste was still in use, along with Corry's Weed-Death with its emblem of a skull and the cheery marketing line: 'Better than arsenic. Highly recommended by the Royal Horticultural Society.' Vivid names such as 'Weedicide' and 'Eureka', were introduced with the usual flamboyant product claims. My favourite is: 'Radioliser radio-active lawn tonic for land... 1lb cannister promises to make your lawn weed free and velvet like. This is fact not fiction... [it] deposits a fine layer of every "food" which fine grass requires, plus the wonderful Radio-active material which produces the rich, blue-green colour...'

Claims were bizarre and contradictory. For instance, the makers of Glymiel Jelly were urging, 'Don't let gardening ruin your hands', while Lever Brothers were recommending Vim, of all things, to clean hands. A 1920 advertisement for Vim added that it was just as good for cleaning kitchen tables, floors, windows, glass and enamelware.

A late 1920s' advertisement for weed-killer trumpets the fact that it was free from arsenic but does so in terms of animal, rather than human, safety. Company names such as International Toxin Products, speak volumes about contemporary gardening culture. The more neutral name 'Cuprinol' is one of the few to have survived.

More familiar still, the John Innes Institute produced its first composts in the 1940s. At last gardeners could buy balanced, sterilized composts designed for seedlings or potting rather than having to mix them themselves. At around the same time the first standardized fertilizer appeared. National Growmore contained nitrogen, potash and phosphate in equal proportions at a low price. Alternative fertilizers included domestic compost (compost heaps started to become popular in the 1940s) and human sewage sold by local councils.

Gardeners Feel the Squeeze

Ready-mixed composts and fertilizers were symptoms of the domestic service labour shortage. Labour-saving devices became increasingly important as garden work was trimmed down to the essentials. By 1914, cucumber straighteners (glass tubes or wooden boxes that were hung around the developing fruit) had been abandoned, along with a host of fiddly garden detail that would once have been carried out by battalions of

Right: Gardeners' Chronicles small ads in 1938 show single men in demand over women. If the gardener was married, his wife was usually expected to work in his employer's house.

gardeners. Men who had served in the trenches, alongside their officers, were reluctant to step back into the servant class. In fact, the whole system and hierarchy of Victorian gardening had already started to crumble when the all-powerful head gardener fell from his throne. Garden owners had less money to spend after the agricultural depression of the 1880s, and after the First World War even those with money had difficulty recruiting gardeners. The wages offered in advertisements before and after the First World War highlight the fact that hiring a gardener had become a much more expensive business.

Some garden owners bucked the trend completely. In the 1920s at Snowshill Manor Charles Wade brought in an untrained garden helper precisely so that he, Charles, could have the garden he wanted without being bullied by a trained gardener!

Mainstream garden owners continued to demand 'strong young men' with good references and experience. One advertised for a gardener who could 'understand a Dennis mower' and 'drive'. Others specify no children, or want a wife as a 'cook general', while some advertisements put the word MAN in bold capital letters, presumably to prevent one of

JULY 23, 1938.

PRIVATE.

WANTED, HEAD GARDENER of 4. Married, under 50; good references and long experience essential.—VISCOUNT SIDMOUTH, Up-Ottery Manor, Honiton.

WANTED, HEAD GARDENER of two for garden of choice shrubs and plants. Hardly any vegetables or glass. Motor mower and occasional scythe. Wages, 45/- weekly and cottage.—REV. PROFESSOR LYTTEL, Nyewoods, Chilworth, Southampton.

HEAD WORKING GARDENER wanted for Norfolk where about four are kept; must be over 35 years, good constitution, married. Thoroughly experienced in all branches of horticulture, both indoors and outside. Apply, with full particulars and wages required.—G. S. JOSLIN, Letton Hall Home Farm, Shipdham, Norfolk.

WANTED, reliable SECOND GARDENER, for inside; cottage provided; not suitable for children.—KIRKLAND, Gardens, Hestercombe, Taunton, Somerset.

WANTED, SECOND of 4, experienced inside and out; married, no children; wages 36/- and lodge.—SIMS, 15, Clewer Village, Windsor.

WANTED, highly experienced FOREMAN for Pleasure Grounds. Only a keen, energetic man with first-class references from well-known gardens need apply. Good wages with bothy and attendance.—Apply, N. REID, Eastwell Park Gardens, Ashford, Kent.

WANTED, strong, Inside FOREMAN, capable plant and fruit grower; good decorator; wages 42/- weekly; bothy, 6/- extra duty. Full particulars, experience, etc.—C. McINROY, Brocket Gardens, Welwyn, Herts.

WANTED, Inside FOREMAN, married, wages £2 and cottage. Apply, with references and full particulars, to LEWIS, Minterne Gardens, Dorchester.

EXPERIENCED GARDENER, under 40 required, understanding kitchen garden routine; must be able to drive car (occasionally); garden boy kept; single man preferred, as only lodgings available at present; 45/- weekly. Write SIR ROBERT DUNLOP, Sandleford Grove, Newbury.

WANTED, experienced MAN, single, for kitchen garden and pleasure grounds; state age, wage, reference; no bothy.—Apply HEAD GARDENER, Oakover Gardens, Ticehurst, Sussex.

WANTED, single MAN, experienced in kitchen garden and lawns, no bothy.—HEAD GARDENER, The Chantry, Elstree, Herts.

WANTED, experienced MAN for glass; thorough knowledge vines, usual fruit and plants, good decorator; age not under 27; wages, 42/-, rising after 6 months if satisfactory 45/-; modern bothy, attendance; duty once in 4 weeks, 6/-. Head Gardener's recommendation.—F. ABRAHAM, Foxwarren Park, Cobham, Surrey.

WANTED, young MAN for inside and out. Full particulars, references, wages expected.—H. FINCHER, Caldecote Nurseries, Nuneaton.

WANTED, UNDER GARDENER, experienced in propagation and cultivation of fruit trees, able work Auto Culto and sprayer; wages 42/6 and holidays with pay.—PRINCIPAL, Lord Wandsworth Agricultural College, Long Sutton, Basingstoke.

REQUIRED, outside JOURNEYMAN for flower gardens, etc., able to take duty. Wages 33/- per week, bothy.—Full particulars and references to HEAD GARDENER, Mostyn Hall Hardens, Mostyn, Flints.

JOURNEYMAN, single, inside, for Fruit and Plant houses, age about 22 yrs.—Apply with particulars, R. WALLIS, The Gardens, Woburn Abbey, Bletchley.

those new-fangled female gardeners from even dreaming of applying.

Gardeners, too, advertised themselves for positions. The women's advertisements make heart-breaking reading. Unlike the men, who list their demands – perks and a minimum wage – the women leave their advertisements open-ended, clearly grateful for anything that they were offered. This is typical: 'Young Lady BSc Hort. desires practical post in garden. Some experience. Can drive a car.'

As always, working conditions for gardeners varied enormously. Long working days, minimal food, low wages and even a seven-day week are recorded through to the end of the Second World War, despite the efforts of the British Gardeners' Association, formed in 1904 'to promote the interests of gardeners, regulate their wages and hours of working'. The following year Kew's director, Sir William Thiselton-Dyer (who certainly had an axe to grind over wage levels), poured scorn on the idea: 'I do not think that it would be possible to bring the scattered units of the gardening profession under the control of anything like a trades-union.'

He was right – collective action was not possible among poorly paid gardeners spread thinly across the country, even though Britain had a rapidly growing labour movement. Eight million people would be signed up as trade unionists by the 1920s; the first Labour government would be in office by 1924, and two years later the General Strike would almost bring the country to a standstill.

The British School of Landscape Architecture and Horticulture tried to do its bit in 1930 by advertising an £85 course for 'male and female students'. It dangled the following carrot to drum up trade: 'Your potential earnings in a normal working career of 50 years are as follows: Assistant gardeners £5,000; Parks Foreman or head gardener £9,000; Landscape gardener £25,000; Horticultural instructor £30,000...Specialist landscape contractor £250,000.'

Many garden owners continued to offer terms that were not dissimilar to those of their Victorian predecessors. One owner in 1950 Charlbury, Oxfordshire, for instance, wanted a young single gardener 'for a private pleasure ground' who could manage glasshouses. The terms were £4 10s a week (if the man was over 21) and a bothy, 'which is attended daily except Sunday by woman to cook etc. and is shared by three other single men. Boarding costs 15/- approx a week.'

Left: Television gardening begun in 1936 with its first presenter, Mr Middleton, in bow tie and three-piece suit.

Above: Fred Streeter,
pictured here in 1946,
broke the formal mould
of television presenters.

Garden Broadcasts

It seems extraordinary that while men
were still being offered Victorian working
conditions, radio and, later, television were
becoming an influential part of everyday life.
In the 1920s the gardener and writer Marion
Cran began her radio series *Garden Talks*.
By 1930 the BBC, with its monopoly of the
airwaves, had three million licensees – and,
therefore, a considerably larger potential
audience. In 1947 the first version of
Gardeners' Question Time was broadcast – and
its audience grew quickly to over a million.

It began in the 1940s as a monthly question
and answer panel game broadcasting to
Northern Ireland with the title *How Does Your
Garden Grow?* It wasn't until the 1950s that it
broadcast nationally, every week, and changed
its name to *Gardeners' Question Time*. The
original panel included Bill Sowerbutts and
Fred Loads, and was chaired by Robert Stead.

Television gardening began in 1936,
when Cecil Middleton sketched pruning
instructions on a blackboard. The programme
had no name that year, but the following year
Mr Middleton's broadcasts were called *In Your
Garden* and later *In Our Garden*.

After a break for the war, garden
broadcasting returned in 1948 when Fred

Streeter helped to front *In Your Garden* and became the first presenter to appear in shirtsleeves! He had begun his working life at the age of twelve, leading a pony-powered mowing machine in the grounds of Petworth House, in West Sussex, where he eventually became head gardener. His starting pay was 3s 6d a week – about 17p. He went on to become a star, the first of the great BBC presenters, who were to wield massive influence from then onwards.

Television gardening had begun its journey to meteoric power and influence – but magazine publishing was in the doldrums. Photography was used to dismal effect in most early twentieth-century magazines, with the notable exception of *Country Life*. Pictures were unfocused or they illustrated plants or scenes that did not merit the attention of a lens. Spartan pictures of 'a box of carnation cuttings' make a sharp contrast to today's over-glamorized garden photographs. Then there was colour. A few contemporary colour pictures were taken of Jekyll's garden at Munstead Wood in Surrey, for instance, but they were rarely reproduced in colour. One leading journal included a black and white photograph optimistically captioned 'a colour scheme for the herbaceous border'.

Above: Gertrude Jekyll's garden at Munstead Wood, Surrey – possibly captured by Herbert Crowley for Country Life in 1912.

5 Modernity and Festivity
New Horizons in the Mid Twentieth-century Garden

Opposite: In 1926 Naumkeag, the iconic New England garden in the USA, showed the future for concrete with these blue steps linking the kitchen and ornamental gardens.

Gardening would take a while to recover from its association with wartime hardship and the Dig for Victory campaign. Even the 1960s, Flower Power movement was more to do with protest politics than plants – other than cannabis. The curious lull in mid twentieth-century garden innovation was partly economic – most large garden owners could barely afford to maintain their existing plots, let alone create new ones. Also, as we shall see, it had to do with the fact that a generation of star designers were seduced away from domestic gardens...by the bulldozer.

1950
Geranium 'Johnson's Blue' named after Welsh market gardener Arthur Johnson

1951
Festival Gardens open
Rosemary Verey moves to Barnsley

1952
C. E. Lucas Phillips's *The Small Garden* on its 17th impression

1953
Structure of DNA discovered by James Watson and Francis Crick
Queen Elizabeth II crowned
Edmund Hillary and Tenzing Norgay climb Everest
Sylvia Crowe makes the Penicillin rose garden
Harold Hillier begins his collection of hardy woody plants

1954
'Queen Elizabeth' rose raised in the USA

1955
Independent television begins broadcasting
Gardening Club broadcast
Graham Stuart Thomas's *Old Shrub Roses* published

1956
Maria Callas makes her debut at the Metropolitan Opera

1957
Geoffrey Jellicoe makes the Sky Garden
John Osborne writes *Look Back in Anger*

All the same more people than ever owned gardens – and a new generation needed some easy way to distinguish their gardens from gloomy wartime plots. As the first chink appeared in the cloud of post-war austerity an old material was reinvented for this new world: concrete. As an industrial material, concrete was the antithesis of the Arts and Crafts ideal – and yet it had a fine pedigree. The Egyptians and Romans used it; in eighteenth-century Britain, Eleanour Coade mixed a version to make her prized garden statuary; and a century later, magnificent Pulhamite rock gardens were built from concrete, as described in Chapter 2. Above all, it was cheap and easy to use, and now it came into its own.

Outside Britain, from the early twentieth century, concrete was being used in seminal gardens. At Naumkeag in Massachusetts, Fletcher Steele used it to make the iconic Blue Steps through the birch woods to join the upper garden to the kitchen garden. Without concrete, the subtly sloping edges of the steps would have been impossible. The 1925 Paris Exposition included a garden of concrete trees, and in 1928 Gabriel Guevrékian made a concrete garden of squares and rectangles, set at various levels, into a prow-like triangle of the Villa Noailles garden in the south of France. The planting was minimal but the

colours were bold – red concrete, blue mosaic and the rest white. This chunk of modern garden first appeared in a couple of Paris exhibitions, thus extending its influence. Then there were Roberto Burle Marx's muscular South American plantings, many set into concrete terraces, photographs of which were published in books and magazines in Britain.

The point about concrete in the 1950s was that, for once, it was used in its own right rather than being made to look like stone. In Britain, the Cement and Concrete Association fanfared the material's renaissance with some innovative gardens and sculptures at Wexham Springs, a park near Slough. Work began in 1959 and included concrete-edged beds and various types of paving and wall sections, intermingled with traditional features, such as lawns and rose arches. Sylvia Crowe made a town water garden. Sculptures such as *Vortex* used innovative techniques to show off concrete's versatility, while the *Corn King* and *Spring Queen* showed concrete at its most exuberant.

Concrete's popularity was the result of far more than clever marketing by the Cement and Concrete Association. It was an ideal material for the fluid shapes favoured by a new generation of landscapers and designers. Two

Right: Concrete seemed to liberate garden design. In the 1920s Gabriel Guevrékian used concrete for his cubist courtyard, while in Wexham Springs near Slough (opposite) concrete took myriad forms, including these sculptures.

Opposite: Brazilian Roberto Burle Marx put the soul into the modern garden using mass plantings with curving lakes and concrete terraces. This is his 1953 garden design at Canoas House, Rio de Janeiro, Brazil.

years before the association started its gardens, the great British landscape architect Geoffrey Jellicoe made his euphoric 'Sky Garden' on the roof of Harvey's store in Guildford, with circular concrete islands and concrete planters dotted about in a pool that reached the outer limits of the roof. A cascade roared down three storeys on one side of the building, although that particular feature lasted only two years. The main roof garden was reconstructed in the late twentieth century, by which time a lift-shaft casing had erupted in the middle of the garden. The architect in charge of the re-vamp, Gerry Lytle, consulted Jellicoe, who was sanguine about whatever changes needed to be made. 'It's only a roof garden,' he told Lytle, and also mentioned that he felt that this was the job that launched him on the road to commercial success. Jellicoe's design was revolutionary and, typically, inspired by ideas and events far beyond the garden wall. According to Lytle, Jellicoe wanted to create a seaside atmosphere so that visitors could feel as if they were on holiday as they ate ice cream and sipped tea in the roof garden café. Concrete stepping stones let visitors 'paddle' without getting wet, and a telescope on the upper level added another seaside reference. If the seaside provided one inspiration, another came from the recently launched first *Sputnik*, and yet more from the influences that shaped

so much of Jellicoe's work: Surrealism, the Pre-Raphaelites, Versailles, chess, Le Corbusier, Pablo Picasso, Carl Jung and Albert Einstein.

Jellicoe designed for a handful of small domestic gardens, too, including his neighbours' long, thin garden (160 x 17ft) in north London. Also, as part of the Festival of Britain in 1951, he created a simple plot of square concrete paviors and two beds for a 20ft square garden. That tiny plot helped show how concrete could be used in a new generation of gardens.

In the 1970s he made Shute House garden in Dorset, with its rill and musical cascade formed out of copper V shapes set into concrete, which caused the water to make various sounds as it fell. The cascades have launched a thousand magazine covers.

A decade later Jellicoe was at work at Sutton Place, near Wisley, creating one of the few great original landscapes of the twentieth century. It included a black-painted swimming pool garden, 'The Miró Mirror', with concrete islands reflecting his friend Joán Miró's work; the Magritte Avenue, with its 3-D *trompe l'oeil*; and the vast walled paradise garden brimming with antique and contemporary references.

Jellicoe was one of a handful of designers to use concrete with style and sophistication. However, the clean-lined designs they were coming up with, such as Sylvia Crowe's iconic ring-shaped concrete planters, were usually found only in smart private gardens or in public parks. Most gardeners took a less restrained approach. Crazy paving, pools, statues, terraces, steps, paths and planters offered a cheap route to garden transformation. Cement and Concrete Association leaflets explained how to make concrete features, while, for gardeners without the DIY knack, builders' merchants supplied concrete paving squares in blue, yellow and pink, a host of concrete ornaments and, eventually, pierced concrete walls.

Modernism Takes Root

Concrete shaped in builders' yards, or by DIY enthusiasts, produced a random selection of ornaments – a squirrel here, a cherub fountain there, mixed in with coloured paving and svelte new planters. And designers who might otherwise have come up with a coherent theme for concrete in small domestic gardens had their sights set on bigger projects. Two reasons for big projects becoming so alluring were the invention of the bulldozer in 1923 and, six years later, the formation of the Institute of Landscape Architects. Bulldozers

could make exciting landscapes quickly and cheaply; the institute gave a focus for young designers who wanted to make their name with prestigious post-war landscaping work on new towns, roads and power stations. Here were opportunities to display brio, and experiment with design principles, on a grand scale. It was hardly surprising that a generation of designers turned away from cash-strapped domestic gardens.

On the whole, innovative design was restricted to public work and a few exceptionally grand or unusual private gardens. By the 1960s, designers such as Sylvia Crowe and Brenda Colvin (who shared an office but were never in partnership as many have since assumed), designed private gardens only for themselves or out of loyalty to old clients. The domestic gardens they built

displayed many of the features that were to become popular at the end of the century: Ali Baba pots; whitewashed garden walls for city basement gardens; shallow pebble ponds for children to play in; simple herb gardens at the kitchen door, and subtle sweeps of perennial planting. In large middle-class gardens, meanwhile, there was little enthusiasm for any dramatic changes. Here the Arts and Crafts style in all its various forms continued to reign triumphant.

One of the few wholesale design philosophies to challenge the Arts and Crafts garden came from the modern movement formulated at the Bauhaus art school in Germany, which was closed by Hitler in 1925. Modern design in gardens is not an easy term to pin down. On one hand there was a belief in respect for place. That could mean leaving the space

Opposite and left: Christopher Tunnard's modern garden at Bentley Wood, Sussex, echoes the grid of the house.

under and around a building untouched or, at most, adding a tranche of naturalized planting. On the other hand, 'modern' came to mean a layout based on shapes inspired by abstract art and planted with sculpture and architectural specimens. For instance, one of the twentieth century's influential designers, John Brookes, made a geometric garden for Penguin Books at Harmondsworth in Middlesex, which was based on a painting by Piet Mondrian. In some respects it is easier to see modern garden design in terms of what it was *not*. It was not to do with herbaceous borders, pretty plantings or tradition. The ideas it embodied helped simplify gardens and challenge the Arts and Crafts monopoly.

A few influential British gardens were made to the modern formula, including those at St Catherine's College, Oxford, and Bentley Wood

on the Sussex Downs. Christopher Tunnard created the Bentley Wood garden in the 1930s to complement architect Serge Chermayeff's house. The garden had a simple terrace of square slabs, and a modest lawn, leading to a large wooden 'picture frame' grid of ten large squares (the lower squares glazed to create a windbreak). This grid framed the neighbouring countryside in a twentieth-century interpretation of the English Landscape movement's use of borrowed views: in other words it incorporated distant landscape into the garden by framing it. At the far side of the frame Henry Moore's *Recumbent Figure*, 'a mediator between a modern house and ageless land', focused on the landscape. Modernism was profoundly influenced by sculpture.

Tunnard's design work influenced a radical minority. In 1939 he was one of those to stage

Below and opposite:
Tunnard's modern legacy
took a while to catch on
but the plants he favoured,
including hostas and
bamboos, had more
instant appeal.

a major exhibition about English landscape, and he was the leading propagandist for the modern movement in Britain before emigrating to work at Harvard in the USA. Set against the voluptuous charms of the Arts and Crafts garden, however, his work seemed cold and startlingly devoid of flowers. To my eye, the austere, uncompromising lines of these original modern buildings sit uneasily in Britain's gentle light and undulating landscape, flowers or not. At Bentley Wood there were flower-beds – narrow areas between the terrace and wall – and areas of naturalized plants in the surrounding (planted) birch woodland, but nothing like the colourful arrays of flowers familiar to most British gardeners.

Naturalized plantings had been around since Robinson's day but Tunnard's planting contribution was a selection of bomb-proof, architectural specimens, which became central to a new generation: *Viburnum davidii*; *Pachysandra terminalis*; golden periwinkle, hostas, grasses, bamboos and New Zealand flax.

Thirty years later, in the early 1960s, the Danish modernist architect Arne Jacobsen created both the buildings and the landscape of St Catherine's College, Oxford. It is one of the clearest and least altered statements of modern gardening. Bold sweeps of lawn and rectangular concrete slabs echo the airy rectangular building and set off a Barbara Hepworth sculpture. The planting focused on foliage, form and colour – grasses, perennials and fine trees (Jacobsen was a plantsman). Symmetrical buttresses and flanks of yew matched the buildings' brick walls.

Jacobsen's countryman Preben Jakobsen would apply modern principles to mass housing schemes in the 1960s when he

FESTIVAL OF BRITAIN

FESTIVAL

PLEASURE GARDENS

BATTERSEA PARK · LONDON

Right: Everything about the Festival Gardens, from the programmes and posters to the gardens themselves, seemed fresh and new.

landscaped Span housing estates. In the 1950s, however, most British gardens were not ready for modern design, as designer and writer Peter Shepheard observed: 'The word modern applied to architecture...is already tarnished with suspicion, and one cannot apply it to gardens without at least a gesture of apology'.

Festival Gardens

In 1951 the curtain went up on a tableau of new gardens at the Festival of Britain. The gardens emerged out of the battered remains of Battersea Park and included the Festival Gardens, now restored, and a series of smaller plots that have long since vanished.

During the Second World War the park had been made into allotments and a tent camp with anti-aircraft guns to protect the power station. These grim reminders of the war were replaced by bright, colourful gardens with wide concrete terraces and stairs in pink, cream, white and blue; a grand vista leading up to a great rectangular pool, where water jets shot into the air, and mass-planted rectangular beds set into concrete. It was quite unlike any other garden of the time, although the designers involved, including Russell Page, borrowed from Regency and other styles to make this new look in which old and new styles jostled together. As Page describes in his

seminal book *Education of a Gardener*, the white, bent-wire edging around some of the flower-beds were inspired by an eighteenth-century jardinière; and the festival's blue-and-white striped tent-like shops by an eighteenth-century French watercolour, while the great terraces of concrete tiles had a modern feel.

Page's planting scheme included rhododendrons taken from one of Britain's finest collections of the plants at the Rothschilds' garden, Exbury in Hampshire. Sourcing plants was tricky because food, rather than ornamental plants, had been the priority in post-war Britain. Page wanted to show off the best of British horticulture, so he turned for help to the RHS, who found a man named E. R. Janes, newly retired from Suttons, to round up and care for the plants. The two men's attempts to find 10,000 hostas produced only fifty. As if finding the plants wasn't difficult enough, Page seems to have been concerned about the survival of the plants because he criss-crossed the tulips with a protective barrier of barbed wire.

The gardens were part of the thirteen-acre Festival of Britain site, which housed the ornate Guinness clock embellished with towers and turrets in bold stripes, mogul-esque pavilions, swags of lights, a model railway, an amphitheatre looking on to an ornate stage with a fish-scale roof, the Shell biplane with its bat-like wings, the *Showboat* – a paddle steamer; Chinese lanterns, dodgems, a children's zoo, a model railway, cart rides, a helter-skelter, live reindeers and everything else needed to make a riotous funfair. The design vocabulary was bewilderingly similar to that of today's Disney: it was enough to make a modernist queasy.

Down river, by the Festival Hall, sophisticated gardens by Maria Shephard-Parpagliolo and

Frank Clark included an amoeba-shaped bed set into a pool and planted with ripples of shrubs and herbaceous plants, with a sculpture at the gravelled centre. Nearby, Peter Shepheard's Moat Garden and some of his other plantings used a now familiar palette: the bamboo *Arundinaria nitida* (now *Fargesia nitida* or fountain bamboo); acanthus, gunnera, *Phormium tenax*; *Cordyline australis* and other big, 'architectural' plants, whose charm depends on shape and form rather than flower. In short, he used the types of plants favoured by Tunnard – plants that were to

Below: Phormium tenax *and other bold architectural plants starred in the Festival Gardens, in contrast to the subtle herbaceous plants that dominated most domestic gardens.*

become popular in 1970s. And at the back of the History of the British People Pavilion there was a garden that might have been planted today – it included tree ferns, bamboos, ferns, ivy and birches. Shepheard and Clark also designed cone-shaped concrete planters, with mushroom lights above, to show off massed tulips and other colourful bedding.

Most of the planting, like the hard land-scaping, was a complete departure. So was the speed at which the gardens appeared. Contemporaries referred to them approvingly as 'instant'.

The Festival Gardens, minus the funfair, were restored in 2003 using Heritage Lottery Funds, although the design was altered in order to combat vandalism. The ghostly outline of Crystal Palace, sketched out by bamboo in 1951, was replaced with high-powered water jets making a similar shape; and Page's exuberant domes and swags beside the tea terrace, the finale to his landscaping, were cut from sheet metal rather than wood as they had been in 1951.

Although the original Festival Gardens were built to last only a year, some sections, such as the Grand Vista Fountain Lake, and some hexagonal- and rectangular-concrete paved terracing, survived until 2002. The restored gardens are intended to be a permanent reminder of this important piece of landscaping, even if they are but a fraction of the astonishing scene that must once have

greeted visitors. In their time they gave a glimpse of the myriad influences that were reshaping gardens for a future generation. Or, as Sylvia Crowe put it in 1958:

[The garden] shows distant descent from the English landscape garden, overlaid with the Robinson–Jekyll tradition of planting, and a strong strain of Japanese influence, while the impulse of the Bauhaus school of architecture gave it a twist towards a new use of free form.

Crowe's contemporary, the landscape architect Brenda Colvin, interpreted and simplified this tidal wave of new ideas for the domestic garden at her home at Filkins in Gloucestershire, where Hal Moggridge today continues the landscape practice. Her garden,

Little Peacocks, includes scant hard landscaping beyond Cotswold stone boundary walls. A serpentine lawn gives an illusion of space and leads through to a second lawn with a central patch of blue anemones and a few snake's-head fritillaries. The wild daffodils here were rescued from the great ash mounds near Selby in Yorkshire that Colvin landscaped. Trees and shrubs separate one area from another, and massed herbaceous plantings give the garden interest without fussiness. I think of this garden as a subtle English version of Roberto Burle Marx's vast South American plantings.

All the same, Little Peacocks is the exception – after all, it was made by a professional for herself. The majority of the garden world was

Opposite and above: Battersea's new gardens were a flamboyant departure from nineteenth-century public parks.

Opposite: Percy Thrower was
the first star of the television
gardening programme
Gardeners' World, which
originally began life as
Gardening Club in 1955.

stagnant, as the historian Miles Hadfield observed in 1954:

Following the eclipse...in the 1939–45 war, no substantial new thought has been added to the art and craft of garden making. But the application of mechanical devices to save man-power, the development of a range of chemicals to kill every known kind of pest, insect and vegetable...has revolutionized garden technique – and introduced unforeseeable new hazards. Plant breeding, particularly in the forcing-ground of the Californian climate, has greatly increased the gardener's material. ...even more important, the numbers of small-ish houses with gardens attached have introduced the pleasures and pains, and ultimate satisfaction of gardening to myriads who have never before experienced them.

And that was the key – small houses run by householders who went out to work.

Books for the Busy

Gardening needed a new, cost-effective, labour-saving approach. The middle classes had to do the garden themselves in between going to the office or raising a family without the domestic help enjoyed by a previous generation. This new dynamic was served by two popular books.

C. E. Lucas Phillips's *The Small Garden*, first published in 1952, had been reprinted seventeen times by 1988. Lucas Phillips was typical of the new generation of middle-class amateur gardeners, as he was happy to confess: 'I myself began gardening just fifty years ago in complete ignorance, making my first attempt by sowing sweet pea seed six inches deep under an elm tree, and having to contend with the problems of catching the 8.30 a.m. daily.'

Lucas Phillips defines a small garden as being one acre, while admitting that typical suburban gardens were 'much smaller'. Either way, he writes, most of the owners of these small gardens had weekly help from a jobbing gardener, who was 'a mixed blessing'. He insists that jobbing gardeners should never be let loose with secateurs, even quoting Milton to make the point: 'blind Fury with th' abhorred shears that slits the thin-spun life'.

His own garden was a classic 1950s' plot. It was highly plant orientated, with conifers and heathers; red, yellow and pink roses; a crazy paving path edged with dwarf pinks and thymes; lawn clipped to within an inch of its life; and a rose pergola with yellow helianthemum Jewel and roses Iceberg and Danse de Feu in the background. However, his

highly practical approach covered every aspect of gardening, from the ornamental to the productive, making his book, apart from the chemical advice, a handy manual even today.

If Lucas Phillips's book was influential, David Hessayon's revolutionized writing on gardening. He is a botanist, soil scientist and accomplished gardener, who published *Be Your Own Gardening Expert* in 1959. This was followed by a now familiar list of titles, including *Be Your Own Greenhouse Expert*, *Be Your Own Rose Expert* and so on – now known simply as the 'Expert' guides. What made them different from Loudon's comprehensive encyclopaedia of a century earlier, and Lucas Phillips's narrative advice, was that the Experts conveyed all their information as a series of diagrams and pictures, each accompanied by brief text. They were excellent, basic handbooks with no further pretension. The information they contained was good and up to date, and their object was simply to serve the reader rather than, as with certain nineteenth-century writers, to score points against rival gardener writers. They jettisoned a lot of gardening's mystique. The Experts did not assume knowledge of Latin or of gardening terms, such as 'mulch'. They explained everything. Above all, they were

Opposite: The Sir Harold
Hillier Garden and
Arboretum, Hampshire,
includes eleven national
collections, with oak
amongst them.

relatively cheap, they were light enough to
be taken into the garden as a pruning crib or
whatever, and they could be bought from
many nurseries – unlike any other books at
the time. Since 1958 the Experts have been
translated into seventeen languages and have
sold over 43 million copies worldwide.

These books were manuals for a world where
time and space had diminished, but the
ultimate expression of garden shrinkage was
the garden-in-a-bottle – a carboy, or large
round glass container, in which foliage
was cultivated by forks tied to sticks. My
grandfather had one – as well as his large
garden! Bottle gardens appeared at Chelsea in
the 1950s and took off in the 1960s, but they
were not as revolutionary as they appeared.
The Victorians had an equivalent – a sort of
Wardian case, which was developed into a
terrarium of increasingly elaborate design.

Media

By this time it was not only books and the
increasingly unstuffy gardening press that
were influencing amateur gardeners.
Television had seduced the nation. The
forerunner of today's massively successful
Gardeners' World began life as *Gardening Club*
in 1955, when it broadcast from the roof
garden at Lime Grove Studios, London. It was

presented by Percy Thrower. The first female
presenter, Frances Perry, author of *The Woman
Gardener*, started work in the 1950s, and soon
afterwards Thrower started his live gardening
slots on *Country Calendar*.

By the 1960s a third of the population
regularly watched television in the evenings.
Gardeners' World began broadcasting in 1968
and has maintained its position as the flagship
gardening programme ever since, regularly
making household names of the presenters.

Even newspapers were catching on to the new
enthusiasm. In 1950 *The Times*, which still
carried advertisements on its front page,
published a threepenny supplement called
'The Survey of Gardening'.

Special Plant Passions

A symbol of gardening's accelerating
popularity was the Chelsea Flower Show's
Great Marquee, which first appeared in 1951.
It was a vast structure, with 6.8 acres of canvas
covering 3.4 acres of ground and weighing 65
tons. The massive, stifling tent, a much-loved
and familiar centrepiece of the show, survived
until the end of the twentieth century, when it
was replaced by light, airy pavilions. These in
turn were replaced in 2004 by a single PVC
Great Pavilion, covering an area the size of

two football pitches. The contents remained the same – plants of enviable quality and, in some cases, great novelty.

For many gardeners, a passion for plants continued to dictate the shape and form of the garden, whatever swanky designers were doing. Increasingly, however, plants were being used in new ways. Instead of imposing a set formula of planting on any garden, whatever its situation, gardeners were beginning to tailor their planting to their own needs – or to those of their plots.

Low-maintenance planting was the theme of Roy Hay's *Gardening the Modern Way*, in which he recommended ground cover for new-style gardens. The importance of ground cover grew with the century, and in 1970 Graham Stuart Thomas came out with a book devoted to the subject. Margery Fish's most famous book, *Gardening in the Shade* (first published in 1964), explained exactly what its title suggested – a breakthrough after years when shady areas were effectively ignored. Design is not a strong theme in any of her books; instead, typically for the time, she focused on naturalistic planting schemes, which always conjured up alluring pictures:

There is no better example [of woodland gardens] to follow than the Savill Garden in Windsor Great Park. There the stream winds under the trees, it is widened here and there and gives glimpses of the garden stretching away into the distance. There are bridges and shallow waterfalls, and irises and primulas, Lysichiton and other bog plants growing at the edge of the water look absolutely natural.

Another author and plantswoman, Beth Chatto (who started White House Barn garden in 1960), is renowned for having turned her tricky, dry site in Essex to great advantage by using it as an experimental garden for drought-tolerant plants. Phyllis Reiss continued a more traditional planting of garden rooms packed with colour-coordinated borders at Tintinhull, the National Trust's property in Somerset, later taken over and developed by the plantswoman and garden historian Penelope Hobhouse.

Roses were still among the nation's best-loved plants – the membership of the Royal National Rose Society was roughly double that of the RHS. Shrub roses in particular were popular thanks to Graham Stuart Thomas's 1955 book, *Old Shrub Roses*. In 1953 Dame Sylvia Crowe put roses into a contemporary setting when she designed the bold, simple Penicillin rose garden in Oxford, just outside the Botanic

Below: The devastating insecticide DDT was the chemical of choice for many mid-century gardeners – despite warnings from the RHS.

gardens, with a framework of yew and box coloured by roses and magnolias.

The vogue for woody plants had been growing steadily since the inception of the great woodland gardens at the start of the twentieth century and the increase in the number of smaller trees collected or bred by nurserymen with an eye on the small-garden market. In 1953 woody material was gathered together by Sir Harold Hillier, who started a Hampshire nursery offering every tree or shrub that is hardy in the UK. Today that nursery has become the Sir Harold Hillier Garden and Arboretum, a 180-acre living catalogue of 40,000 plants. It was the culmination of a crusade begun by his grandfather Edwin Hillier and his father Edwin Lawrence Hillier.

The Modern Garden Shed

This wealth of plants needed to be maintained and, now that gardens had to be run with little or no help, chemicals were seen as the obvious solution. Here, it seemed, was a simple and efficient way to keep pests and disease under control and plants well fed and healthy. Faith in chemical solutions had been fostered during the war, when the Dig for Victory campaign was accompanied by a belief that chemicals carried most of the answers for an

KYBOSH D.D.T. SPECIAL Garden Spray for Caterpillar, Beetle, etc. Safe and easy to use.
½ pint (12½ glns.) 2/3

expanding population with diminishing access to imported food. DDT was in demand by British gardeners. A lone voice of warning came from the RHS, which cautioned that not enough was known about DDT's long-term effects on warm-blooded creatures. It was ignored: the chemical had wiped out malaria in various parts of the Empire and it had been used with abandon throughout the war, so why not in peacetime too?

While Arther Billitt, a chemist who had retired from Boots, sustained the chemical gardening tradition with regular television appearances, Lucas Phillips wrote out the chemical agenda for a generation: chlordane for worm casts; BHC for leather jackets; gassing for moles; ICI's organo mercury compound, Verdasan, for soil-bound diseases (dropped by ICI in the 1980s); systemic fungicide for fruit trees; tar wash in winter; Fenitrothian against sawfly and codlin moth; and a soil treatment, Bromophos, against carrot fly. In 1958 paraquat and diquat were introduced as herbicides. Chemical fertilizers and substances labelled with the newly coined term 'pesticides', including DDT and lead arsenate, were usually used without protection. Few knew about their harmful side-effects, and they were advertised using vocabulary that now appears contradictory. For instance, 'Velvetone' was extolled as an 'organic' lawn conditioner – and it was made by International Toxic Products.

Plastic, like chemicals, transformed aspects of garden maintenance. Plastic pots eventually brought down the cost of running a garden, both financially and in terms of ricked backs. And clear plastic sheeting made garden frames cheaper and easier to manoeuvre. Three-foot rolls of clear plastic Plybel were advertised at 8s 9d a yard for garden frames. New materials were changing the way the garden looked, as well as the way in which it was maintained.

Terracotta

Cheap new materials gave certain traditional materials new status. Terracotta, fashionable nearly a century earlier, was back – despite the fact that traditional terracotta flowerpots were gradually being replaced by plastic. Ornamental pots and pottery had become chic among a smart set, who, by the late 1950s, took holidays on the Mediterranean. The vogue for terracotta was heightened by the style king Terence Conran and the great cook Elizabeth David, who made terracotta pots part of any smart kitchen. In Essex the influential architect Frederick Gibberd was creating an unusual garden that depended on sculptural forms, including terracotta pots, for focus and interest – it is being restored as I write. And Luis Barragán, the great Mexican architect, used groups of utilitarian pots to decorate corners of his terraces and add interest on a human scale to his monumental, brightly coloured water features at places such as his San Cristóbal stables.

Post-war Gizmos

A radio-controlled mower appeared in *The Times*' garden of tomorrow at the Chelsea Flower Show in 1959. It was made by H. C. Webb and, according to a report in *Gardeners Chronicle*, it 'moved around the lawn on its own' and caught the public imagination. However, this was a prototype and, since it was not mentioned subsequently, it probably never went into mass production. Instead it epitomized an ideal – a future in which hard graft was carried out by machine.

6 The Room Outside
The Greening of Late Twentieth-century Gardening

Opposite: Hidcote's well-proportioned garden rooms were forerunners of the late twentieth-century room outside.

Prosperity, that excellent gardening tool, went hand in hand with increasing home ownership. In the twenty years from 1970 to 1990 consumer spending on gardens rose from £119 million a year to £1,435 million. Expensive (and sometimes innovative) garden schemes were encouraged by Nigel Lawson's 1986 cap of 40 per cent on top-rate taxpayers. The Chelsea Flower Show, a barometer of gardening's popularity, had to limit visitor numbers after a show in the 1980s attracted a massive 247,000 people, which made it all but impossible to see the gardens. For the first time RHS members had to pay for tickets. Ten thousand of them resigned as a result.

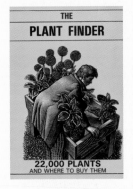

THE
PLANT FINDER

22,000 PLANTS
AND WHERE TO BUY THEM

Below: One of the first garden centres in Britain was opened by Charles Notcutt in 1958.

Instant Gratification

By the end of the 1970s garden centres had created a new generation of gardeners, and begun today's out-of-town shopping trend. Before the arrival of garden centres most gardeners ordered bare-rooted plants from nurseries and bought their tools, hoses, seeds and so on from high street hardware or floristry shops. This needed both planning and plant knowledge. Customers at garden centres needed neither – they could see the plants they were about to buy. Tools, containers, compost, irrigation systems and chemicals could be bought at the same time as plants. This one-stop shop made gardening fun and unthreatening – a change from having to plough though sparsely illustrated, Latin-heavy nursery catalogues.

The origin of garden centres goes back to the 1950s, when British nursery owners imported the new shopping concept from the USA and Australia. Wyevale and Waterers were two of the movement's pioneers, and the story of Notcutts is typical. In 1958 Charles Notcutt opened a garden centre half a mile from his shop in Woodbridge, Suffolk, to expand the range of seeds and tools he sold there to include bulbs and plants. The plants had hessian-wrapped root balls, or they were heeled in so that customers could select for

themselves. Staff were on hand to help dig out plants if necessary. Notcutt, who in 1986 was so worried at first about whether or not customers would trek the extra half-mile to his garden centre that he stopped capital expenditure for three years. Fortunately, the business prospered, particularly after the 1971 postal strike, which severely damaged the mail-order nursery business, and in 1986 he became the first chairman of the Garden Centre Association.

Plant containerization was part of the garden centre revolution. Containerized plants could be sold and planted throughout the year instead of being offered only in spring and autumn. Before plastic pots appeared, plants were grown in anything available. Waterers sent their men out to knock on doors around Bagshot asking for old biscuit tins. Further west, Wyevale used jam tins from the NAAFI at RAF Hereford. Notcutts used similar containers but built their first containerization plant – using plastic pots – in the 1970s. It soon expanded to 20 acres. Mechanization and mass production were the keys to success.

Beautiful Backyards

The USA helped to give us garden centres, and it also showed us a new way of seeing and using our gardens. The Hollywood ideal of glamorous, outdoor parties and meals around a swimming pool was a far cry from the worthy joys of an Arts and Crafts garden. The fact that most Britons had to duck in and out of the garden as weather permitted did not dampen the enthusiasm for the new vogue. The smaller size of houses made outdoor living all the more alluring.

The new approach to garden use was captured by the designer John Brookes's 1968 book *The Room Outside*. The title had a democratic, user-friendly ring that chimed with the times. The idea itself was ancient – going back to the medieval *hortus conclusus* or, more recently, to nineteenth-century Elvaston or early twentieth-century Hidcote – but this time round it encapsulated the new attitude to gardens partly inspired by the American designer Thomas Church's 1950s' book *Gardens Are for People*.

On this side of the Atlantic it took Brookes to popularize the idea of the garden as an extension of the house, and as a place to be used by the family and their pets. His influences came from Scandinavia as much as the USA, and although he had yet to travel there, he studied plans and photographs of clean-lined Scandinavian buildings and parks. Brookes was born in 1933, a year after Gertrude Jekyll died, and grew up in an entirely Jekyllian tradition, which gave him a good understanding of the Arts and Crafts garden, as well as a fiery ambition to break away from it.

Above: Decking, a barbecue, a dining table and sun loungers make this 1979 garden at architect Roger Dyer's home a perfect room outside.

Above: Late twentieth-century gardens began to get smaller as leisure time decreased which popularized the use of concrete paving and simple plantings.

In order to make his design ideas accessible, Brookes devised a grid system for garden planning that could be applied by anybody, in any garden, however small. In the many books that followed *The Room Outside*, he went into unapologetic detail about how to construct steps, lay drainage and build a garden from scratch. This technical detail about garden construction and engineering was a departure from planterly books by Jekyll, Fish and Sackville-West, which had been so popular in the early and middle parts of the century, and this 'can-do' approach to garden construction

paved the way for the massively popular DIY stores and garden programmes of today.

Brookes's design school, Denmans in West Sussex, was founded in 1980, and many similar schools opened up a new career path for a generation – I was a Brookes student in 1984. In 1981 he and others founded the Society of Garden Designers, to provide a forum and regulating body for designers, and in the 1990s he ran some of Kew's first design courses.

The concept of the outside room began to mingle with the stylish ideas that the British were picking up from Mediterranean holidays. The gardener and writer Anne Scott-James's contemporary description of an ideal 1977 garden paints a vivid picture:

'Here...the owner re-lives the holidays he has spent in southern Europe; here he paves and plants in the Mediterranean manner; here he quaffs *vin rosé* and serves scampi Provençal. A patio is as much a dream garden as Chatsworth or Sissinghurst and gives far less trouble.'

Scott-James's tasteful outside room was one incarnation. Others were fashioned by the interesting ornaments and gadgets available at the newly emerging garden centres, and described here, in 1969, by the designer and writer Peter Shepheard:

The mode consists of a very strange collection of elements which have an outrageous incongruity with each other and with all modern situations: Cotswold stone retaining walls; vaguely Spanish wrought-iron gates; 'crazy' paving, nowadays often coloured yellow, green and pink; tiny irregular ponds, now usually of pale blue fibreglass, fed by streams of improbable source; gnomes, fairies and animals, usually plastic, of vaguely Neapolitan colouring; dwarf Cypress trees...

Moulded fibreglass ponds – in blue, white, yellow or avocado – often had a 'rockery' at one end, made from the pond excavations, with chunks of concrete or stone added. A stream (created by pumped, circulating water) meandered through the 'boulders'. Water gardening, promoted by specialists such as Stapeley Water Gardens in Cheshire, boomed as the number of associated gadgets increased – affordable pumps and fountains, butyl liners and, for the tiny garden, wall-mounted water features.

New materials, such as plastic, nylon and aluminium, had a massive impact. Sun loungers and chic, collapsible chairs that could withstand weather and be carried in and out of the shed easily were as ubiquitous in Britain as they were in the south of France. A classic early 1970s' lounger – one that I remember from my childhood – had an aluminium frame criss-crossed with coloured plastic tubing. It left interesting patterns on sunbathers' thighs.

Decking became an important part of the room outside, along with another American-inspired feature – the swimming pool. Neither was ideal for Britain's climate, but decks became more user friendly with the introduction of ridged, tanalized timber, which prevented decks from becoming too slippery. The popularity of pools was a reaction partly to polluted rivers and lakes and partly to movie images of sun-kissed nirvana beside the pool. In 1964 the *Architectural Review* estimated that ten thousand new pools had been built in private gardens in Britain.

Gardens were becoming chic – and they acquired wide-screen glamour from Peter Greenaway's 1982 film *The Draughtsman's Contract*, set in Groombridge Place, with its seventeenth-century house and its curious 'drunken garden' of topiary.

*Above: Architectural plants,
such as cordyline, euphorbia
and mahonia, dominated
chic gardens.*

Plant Obsession

Garden centres, and a vogue for simple,
massed planting, killed off many nurseries and
for a time even threatened the UK's plant
heritage. Two saviours came to the rescue.
Chris Philip published *The Plant Finder*, which
listed over 70,000 plants and where to find
them. It first appeared in 1987 and has been
updated annually. Eight years earlier, in 1979,
the National Council for the Conservation of
Plants & Gardens was started by the RHS to
'conserve, document, promote and make
available Britain's great biodiversity of garden
plants for the benefit of horticulture,
education and science'. This crusading work
was carried out by volunteers such as Dianne
Allison, a nurse and single mother, who
assembled the National Collection of
Polemonium (Jacob's Ladder) at her semi-
detached home on an estate near Consett,
County Durham.

For mortal gardeners, 'architectural' plants,
such as *Euphorbia characias* subsp. *wulfenii*,
cordylines, caster oil plants and mahonia,
were in favour during the 1970s. Climbers,
including actinidia, ivy and vines, clambered
over the boundaries to add privacy to the new
suburban kingdoms. Island beds of perennials
and conifers appeared, inspired by Alan Bloom,
the Norfolk nurseryman, whose book on the

subject was published in 1975. David Austin's
remontant old-fashioned English roses were
prized and brought roses back into fashion.

On the whole, low-maintenance gardening
was 'in', but there was a voluptuous exception
to the rule. Myles Challis's book *The Exotic
Garden* appeared in 1988 and coined a far
more labour-intensive planting. Using
bamboos, ferns, hardy bananas and palms,
Challis created a jungle in London's East End.
His exotic garden, and his book, were inspired
by Henry Cooke's *A Gloucestershire Wild
Garden*, and became the setting for the film
The Assam Garden. By the 1990s exoticism had
even stolen into the Arts and Crafts garden of
Great Dixter in East Sussex. Christopher Lloyd,
the entertaining and prolific gardening writer
and plantsman, has lived at Great Dixter since
his birth in 1921. His parents, who employed
Edwin Lutyens to design the grounds, were
gardeners, and Christopher's mother, Daisy,
gardened there until she died in 1972. His
father, Nathaniel, died in 1933. In 1994
Christopher ripped out Lutyens's rose garden
and replaced it with a spicy mix of cannas,
dahlias and bananas mingled with the
dancing purple of *Verbena bonariensis*. Shock
horror! The whiff of smelling salts pervaded
the more traditional parts of the gardening
establishment.

Opposite: The dry stream at John Brookes's garden Denmans in Sussex, where grasses mingle with verbascum and other self-seeders.

Dry summers in the latter part of the century, exacerbated by hose-pipe bans, forced new styles into common use: gravel beds, pioneered by Joyce Robinson at Denmans garden in Sussex, were popularized by John Brookes and Beth Chatto, who were also responsible for making Mediterranean planting schemes fashionable. The threatened effects of global warming were now beginning to bite. Ornamental grasses were ideal for the new planting style, and by the 1990s they had become a chic addition to mixed borders, thanks to the Dutchman Piet Oudolf.

For container gardens the universal F1 hybrid winter-flowering pansy revolutionized 1980s' winter displays.

Whatever the planting, a weed-free lawn was still the norm, as Russell Page observed in *The Garden* – the booklet of the V&A's eponymous 1979 exhibition: 'Grass lawns are with us still, technically more perfect than ever, although I rather regret the vanished shabbier kind, where clover and daisies and clouds of blue speedwell and the odd primrose or cowslip flowered.'

But wildlife was about to fight back.

TV and the Green Room

From the late 1960s onwards, bleak news about the harmful side effects of garden chemicals began to turn gardeners green with environmental concern. Rachel Carson's *Silent Spring*, published in the 1960s, made the link between agro chemicals and loss of wildlife. It was the beginning of the end for many garden chemicals, and DDT was banned from the domestic market in 1970, although lindane, another organochlorine, wasn't banned until 1998. Organic gardening, as popularized by television, slowly filled the gap.

In 1976 Percy Thrower's association with the BBC ended shortly after he appeared on ITV advertising garden chemicals. He was the first television gardening presenter to have appeared in colour – and he did so as the *Blue Peter* gardener. In fact, Thrower's departure was more to do with contractual disagreements rather than any greening of the BBC. It was years before television began to look seriously at the alternatives to gardening with chemicals, and when it did the well-ordered world of small-screen gardens was turned on its head. Channel 4's *All Muck and Magic* in 1991 showed gardens in which purpose – the organic production of food and flowers – reigned supreme over style. Most of the series was filmed at the Henry Doubleday

Left: Piet Oudolf's plantings mingle grasses with more traditional herbaceous specimens.

Above: Geoff Hamilton at his garden, Barnsdale, the focus of millions of Gardeners' World fans.

Research Association, the HDRA, in the Midlands.

The HDRA was an organic organization that had opened its 10-acre Ryton Organic Gardens near Coventry in 1985. Thirty years had passed since it began life as Lawrence and Cherry Hills' campaigning project on an Essex smallholding in 1954. Lawrence began by funding his experimental work (on comfrey and organic gardening) with freelance journalism – including an *Observer* column. He started the HDRA in order to spread the organic word and persuade gardeners to carry out organic growing experiments in their own gardens – a tradition that continues today. By the early 1990s the organization opened a second trials ground and garden near Maidstone in Kent, laid out as a journey through garden history.

Organic gardening had a serious image problem. It was a byword for creating ugly gardens – and this put off many mainstream gardeners. Poor funding didn't help the problem any more than such well-publicized practices as using old carpet as weed suppressant. The chaotic appearance of many organic gardens made them an easy target for critics. Even organic gardeners came in for mud-slinging – many were dismissed as sandal-wearing cranks. The HDRA was determined to transform this dowdy image and bring the organic message into mainstream gardening. Ryton created show gardens to demonstrate that an organic garden could be as stylish as a conventionally maintained plot.

It was Geoff Hamilton, presenter of the BBC's *Gardeners' World* for seventeen years, who made green gardening 'normal'. He demonstrated organic gardening methods at Barnsdale, the Rutland garden that he shared with millions of BBC viewers. By the beginning of the 1990s Hamilton had also switched from peat to coir in an attempt to help save ancient peat habitats from being destroyed by the gardening industry. Alan Titchmarsh took up the green gardening theme when *Gardeners' World* moved to his Hampshire garden, Barleywood, after Geoff Hamilton's untimely death in 1996.

Left: Those engaged in chemical warfare needed protection in the battlefield or the greenhouse.

Kew, like the RHS, had been ahead in the green game. Not only was it the first large organization to make a high-profile switch from peat to coir, but as early as 1970, its gardeners had to wear protective overalls when using DDT, paraquat and other weapons of garden warfare. By the late 1980s Kew was using biological pest control in its glasshouses, a method it had first tried in the 1870s.

In fact, there were many who had been trying to spread the green message long before Rachel Carson's *Silent Spring*. At the turn of the seventeenth century Joseph Addison wrote that he'd rather preferred cabbages and other common plants to tender exotics because,

...my garden invites into it birds of the country, by offering them the conveniency of springs and shades, solitude and shelter, I do not suffer anyone to destroy their nests in the spring, or drive them from their usual haunts in fruit-time. I value my garden more for being full of blackbirds than cherries... By this means I have always the music of the season in its perfection...

In the first half of the twentieth century Lady Eve Balfour helped start the Soil Association, whose symbol is awarded to organically grown produce. Even Russell Page, better

known for his internationally acclaimed designs than horticultural know-how, wrote in the early 1960s about the importance of a compost heap to:

...ensure me a regular supply of black humus, since I know of no better way of having a garden relatively free from pests and disease. There are limits to the time, trouble and money I am prepared to spend on spraying my garden with chemical preparations which can so easily destroy nature's subtle balances and, by eliminating one pest, fatally leave the door open for others.

The vogue for ecologically sound gardens, organic gardens and wildlife gardens prospered, and continues to do so, despite dissent from the influential and elegant voice of Robin Lane-Fox, the gardening correspondent of the *Financial Times*. He recommends the use of chemicals as

an accurate and efficient way to give plants the correct quantities of nutrients, and to control pests and disease in gardens. This is what he wrote in the aftermath of the 2001 National Trust gardens conference: '...the summary omitted...my full observations on the control of wildlife in gardens, including the need to kill it in any serious garden of flowers.'

By now the green movement had powerful sponsors, including Prince Charles, who was building an eclectic garden around his Cotswold home, Highgrove. One of his helpers was Lady Salisbury, who had been gardening without chemicals at Hatfield House and Cranborne Manor without any aesthetic compromise. It helped that she was rich enough to afford plenty of labour. With advice from the Marchioness and the HDRA, Prince Charles created a green, wildlife-friendly garden, which included a reed bed filtration system for household sewage. There were plenty of purely aesthetic features, too – a contemporary stumpery; a temple/summer house; plantings by Rosemary Verey; a tree house; and a space-age William Pye water sculpture. Also, along the drive leading up to Highgrove, the prince planted a wildflower meadow with the help of the gardener/ entomologist Miriam Rothschild, a veteran green campaigner.

Wildflower Gardening

For many years Rothschild had been encouraging gardeners to use her wildflower seed mix 'Farmers' Nightmare', but it wasn't until the 1980s that domestic wildflower gardening took off. In 1985 the landscaper/ ecologist Chris Baines brought a garden of wildflowers to Chelsea. It made a big impression at the time. Soon afterwards I was involved in a *Daily Express* garden in which 'weedy' meadow turf had been planted: the reaction of many Chelsea visitors was one of polite bewilderment. Baines's BBC television series, and the accompanying book, showed how to make a wildlife garden in even the tiniest city space. Gardeners were encouraged to see their gardens as oases for wildlife threatened by agrochemicals.

The practicalities of wildflower cultivation were too much for some gardeners, who were caught unawares by high maintenance levels.

Below: Hidcote, in
Gloucestershire, was the
first garden to be taken
over in its own right by
the National Trust.

If only they had heeded Sylvia Crowe's warning earlier in the century: 'For those who believe that a wild garden ends all maintenance problems, it is salutary to remember that, according to Milton, it was the pressure of this work which caused Adam and Eve to work in different parts of the garden and so gave the serpent his opportunity.'

'Wild gardening' in the sense of native planting seemed revolutionary in the 1980s but it could be compared to the garden work of Wordsworth and that of many of the eighteenth century's 'picturesque' landscapers. In the late nineteenth century Oscar Wilde was among a group of Oxford students who planted wildflowers along a road they had

the vogue for native planting had increased awareness about appropriate planting, i.e. about designing gardens in which soil and ecology dictated the plant list.

Nostalgia and Restoration

Two years after Boulger's RHS lecture Edith Holden started her diary of Warwickshire life and illustrated it with delicate watercolours of the wildflowers around her. In 1977, when a facsimile reproduction of her diary was published as *The Country Diary of an Edwardian Lady*, it made an unexpected smash hit and went to seven editions in a matter of months. Nostalgia had been spreading its sepia fingers. Post-war Britain had looked forward to a clean-lined modern space age. London swung, miniskirts climbed sky high and then, abruptly, came an about-turn. Laura Ashley's floral frocks and smocks set the fashion agenda, while Heritage set the cultural agenda.

built. This forerunner of today's motorway wildflower plantings was described by contemporaries as 'far more beautiful than any college garden'. It took the RHS to focus on the long-term problem, however, and at a lecture at the Society in 1904 G. S. Boulger warned about the danger of losing wildflower species. By the end of the twentieth century

The National Trust, formed at the beginning of the century, was at the centre of the heritage industry, although its focus was houses rather than gardens. Hidcote, in Gloucestershire, was the first garden to be taken on by the Trust in its own right. It was accepted in 1948 with advice and financial help from the RHS. There was little money to run it, and Graham Stuart Thomas was brought in to arrange economies. When the gardens opened in 1956, barely 1,000 people visited in the first year. In recent years the number has been as high as 147,000.

In 1965 Westbury Court in Gloucestershire, one of Britain's only intact, formal Dutch gardens, was threatened by developers. The Trust stepped in and, with difficulty, raised £20,000 to buy the place. Restoration money was not forthcoming so, with the help of the newly formed Garden History Society, the Trust set about the restoration on a shoe string, using volunteer labour. It was one of the first major garden restorations in Britain, and it heralded the start of our love affair with old gardens, which had, until then, been poor relations of houses, churches, abbeys and other architectural monuments.

Today the National Trust runs about 200 parks and gardens, and employs three garden curators, a garden historian, three gardens advisers, a garden and parks conservation planner and myriad gardeners (voluntary and professional), all of whom work to the head of gardens, Mike Calnan.

Restoration fever spread across a disparate array of gardens, from glorious, rococo Painswick in Gloucestershire to the trust's extraordinary Biddulph Grange in Staffordshire. Garden history boomed: Kew opened the Queen's Garden to show a seventeenth-century planting; the V&A staged its exhibition 'The Garden'; Rosemary Nicholson founded the Museum of Garden History in the derelict church where the great seventeenth-century plant hunters the Tradescants are buried; English Heritage began their Register of Gardens in order to survey and, where possible, protect important gardens and landscapes; and in 1987 Sotheby's and the RHS mounted a joint exhibition, 'The Glory of the Garden'. In the same year David Wheeler founded *Hortus*, a black and white anomaly in an increasingly slick and glossy magazine market, which took a thoughtful look at gardens. Roy Strong, former director of the V&A, wrote books and articles about British garden history, staged exhibitions and, at The Laskett, the Herefordshire garden he has made with his wife Julia Trevelyan Oman, combined an autobiographical stroll with historical references and a crab apple collection.

Landscape restoration was one thing, planting quite another. Some justified using new cultivars in historic gardens on the grounds that gardeners will always experiment with

Right: Painswick in Gloucestershire is a rare jewel – a rococo garden. It was in the first wave of garden restoration.

The Room Outside **169**

Opposite: Rosemary Verey smartened up her Barnsley House vegetable plot and turned it into a potager. Clients who wanted something similar were told that if they wanted to eat their own vegetables they would have to grow them elsewhere.

new plants. Those who tried to reproduce an exact historic planting faced a problem encountered by a generation earlier – many plant varieties were no longer available, victims of the gradual demise of large nurseries after the First World War.

Gardening for All

Garden centres were offering a far more limited plant palette than the great pre-war nurseries. On the other hand, a greater number of people, from every level of society, were running their own ornamental gardens. The RHS reflected this change in 1975 when *The Journal of the RHS* was renamed *The Garden* and redesigned to educate and encourage gardeners from every walk of life, rather than the landowners, head gardeners and expert horticulturalists who had once commanded most attention from the society. In the 1970s the RHS scrapped the system of fellows and allowed anyone who was prepared to pay the membership fee to join the society. The massive upsurge in garden popularity was consolidated by television, radio, magazines and books. Every aspect of the subject – from horticulture to design – became accessible.

Gardening magazines, once a vehicle for smart opinions and internecine war between head gardeners, were increasingly becoming good

sources of technical and consumer advice. In 1982 two magazines, *Garden Answers* and *Gardening from Which?*, began to feed the need for clear, well-researched information. This was Margaret Thatcher's era of hard work and hard play – limited spare time could not be spent reading long articles for the sake of a few pieces of information.

The Vegetable Plot

In the midst of this time-challenged era, one of the most time-consuming types of garden, the vegetable plot, was back in vogue for the first time since the war. Two BBC series primed the cult: *The Victorian Kitchen Garden* (1987) and *Mr Smith's Vegetable Garden* – Geoffrey Smith's launch pad as a garden presenter.

The craze materialized in two forms: potagers, or ornamental vegetable gardens (perfected by Rosemary Verey at Barnsley House in Gloucestershire) and middle-class allotments. Food scares about high chemical content and, later, genetic modification in shop-bought produce had fuelled the grow-your-own movement. The limited, tasteless range of fruit and vegetables available in supermarkets also stoked interest in home-grown produce. Practical advice about growing vegetables without the help of chemicals came from the HDRA.

Right: The Liverpool Garden Festival in 1984 brought money and employment to the riot-torn city.

This organic organization also provided 'heritage' seed varieties, which produced tasty vegetables or pest-and-disease-resistant crops. They made a delicious change from the huge, insipid varieties bred to win prizes in produce shows. Then a problem emerged. The sale of heritage seed was effectively outlawed by the EU. It was a problem I faced on *The Times* when, in the 1990s, we started a grow-your-own campaign with Heligan Gardens in Cornwall. The Long White Marrow, one of the varieties that had not been EU approved, was a vegetable we wanted to include in the campaign. *The Times*'s lawyers were consulted and sorted out the problem with their usual aplomb. They advised forming a readers' club that would supply 'free' seed to those who had paid their membership fee. It was a daft system – but the readers grew Long White Marrows and nobody attempted to prosecute the newspaper or Heligan Gardens.

Greatly Diminished Gardens

Heligan Gardens were restored in the nick of time, as we shall see in the following chapter, but the first half of the twentieth century had seen the destruction of many great estates. John Harris, a champion of the country house, estimates that in 1955 alone 'one substantial historic house was demolished every two days or so'. With the houses went the gardens. As economic prosperity returned, the influence of 'great' gardens gradually resumed, but the damage had been done. Gardens that survived beyond the 1950s faced serious maintenance problems. At Shrubland Park in Suffolk economies cut the gardening staff from forty to four, and... 'reduced the glowing parterres to roto-scythed grass...the neo-Italian style must depend for its charm only on the main lines of its structure and the detailing of the ballustrading and staircases.'

Left: George Carter's straw pavilions at the Stoke Garden Festival brought eighteenth-century ideas to life in the late twentieth century.

It wasn't only the gardens that were lost – skills and horticultural traditions went with them. Apprentice schemes vanished and horticultural schools closed. One of the few that never faltered, other than during the wars, was the Wisley School of Horticulture, which had been training gardeners since the beginning of the century. The 1980s saw a revival in horticulture courses and schools, and in 1991 the National Trust began an apprentice scheme.

Then gardening was given a fillip from another, unexpected source.

Garden Festivals

After visiting riot-torn Liverpool in July 1981, the secretary of state for the environment, Michael Heseltine, announced his plan for the first garden festival. It was an idea that had been brewing since his fellow MP Sir Philip Goodhart told him about garden festivals on the Continent. Heseltine wanted festivals to regenerate impoverished areas of the country by injecting capital and creating employment, at least in the short term. The Liverpool festival attracted three and a half million people, and became the UK's most visited event of 1984. Stoke-on-Trent's festival in 1986 had seventy theme gardens, a festival hall, a marina and a mass of installations and displays more or less related to gardens over what had been a derelict steelworks. Criticisms of the events came largely from those who did not visit them. For those of us who did, there were plenty of stimulating design ideas mingled with the naff and the silly. I saw my first George Carter installation at the Stoke garden festival – an ornate haystack, based on the eighteenth-century landscaper Batty Langley's idea about incorporating rural references in a formal

The festivals were not the only organizations serving gardeners outside the south-east. Rosemoor Garden in Devon was given to the RHS by Lady Anne Palmer in 1987, thus opening its fine collection of specimen trees to the public. Six years later, Hyde Hall in Essex was donated and now boasts 4,000 drought-tolerant plants. Harlow Carr in Yorkshire, where we built gardens for the television series accompanying this book, is the northern jewel in the RHS crown. It is a cold and exposed site, and, as the curator points out, 'if it will grow here it will grow anywhere'.

Japanese Partners

Festivals and gardens were part of the revival in garden fortunes which, during the 1980s, went hand in hand with a revival in our old love affair with Japanese gardens. This time there was a variation on the oriental theme: the Japanese were as enamoured with our gardens as we were with theirs. Rosemary Verey, John Brookes and Bunny Guinness were among those commissioned to make English gardens in Japan. Then, in 1991, the Kyoto Garden Association made the Japanese garden in Holland Park.

RHS Japan was formed in Tokyo in 1987 after the RHS gave technical and planting advice at Akagi Nature Park's Rhododendron Garden.

landscape or, as Langley put it, 'pleasant meanders' containing 'Haystacks and Wood Piles'. Each to his own – but Carter's designs looked superb. In a curious twist to this story, Heseltine, now a peer known for his fine arboretum in Northamptonshire, completed a magnificent walled garden designed by Carter, in 2003 – although Heseltine only became aware of Carter's work at a recent Chelsea Flower Show.

By 2002 RHSJ had 3,200 members and close links with the UK. Kew continued its historic association with Japan, and Japanese students came to study and work there. A Japanese wildflower meadow appeared at Chelsea, and six internationally renowned Japanese designers built display gardens at Kew. Language barriers created problems when it came to the explanation of the gardens – and the gardens themselves did not sit well in Kew's landscape – but here, at last, were some exciting, contemporary Japanese gardens available to the British gardening public.

Japan was one of many foreign cultures influencing British garden design. Scandinavia, the USA, Spain, Italy, France and South America had also been making their contributions since the mid century. Modified versions of these foreign ideas filtered into domestic gardens from the 1960s, and, happily, the heart-sinking pastiches of 'Japanese' gardens that had infected Britain at the turn of the nineteenth century were not (often) repeated. Landscape and design theory had become more sophisticated – foreign garden design was interpreted rather than copied. Cheap travel, better communication and high-quality photographs of foreign gardens helped the assimilation of foreign design principles.

Gizmos

Hover mowers symbolized the new approach to gardening. They were light, easy to use and simple to store in the smallest space, they looked trendy, and they left none of the sturdy green stripes that characterized an earlier era of gardening. Flymo, invented by Karl Dahlman, began production in the UK in 1965, using technology pioneered six years earlier by the first cross-Channel hovercraft.

Above: Bye-bye stripy lawn, hello the fab Flymo that hangs in a cupboard.

7 Radical Designs
New Departures for a New Millennium

Opposite: Parc André Citroën, Paris, has it all: clean-lined open spaces, intimate enclosures, cool greens, colourful planting and crazy water jets.

Gardens are the new sex, or so the glossy magazines tell us. Gardening is certainly Britain's favourite pastime – and an industry worth £3.5 billion a year. This national passion, fuelled by wealth, leisure and new materials, is creating a generation of revolutionary gardens. And I wonder what the founding fathers of the RHS would have made of them. Vibrant colour is as likely to come from coloured plastic and concrete and pigmented wood preservative as it is from flowers. Contemporary materials have created new features: colourful, hard-wearing polymer flooring; lightweight nylon sails to decorate and shade; fibreglass chill-out pits (the cool version of the summer-house); and aluminium scaffolding terraces.

1991
First Gulf War
First Chaumont-sur-Loire international garden festival

1992
Rio Earth Summit
Garden Writers' Guild formed

1993
Spice Girls release their first single

BBC *Gardeners' World Live* opens at the NEC, Birmingham

1994
Channel Tunnel opens
Osmacote slow-release fertilizer available to domestic gardeners

1995
30 million Internet users worldwide
Heritage Lottery Fund begins

1996
Guy Cooper and Gordon Taylor's *Paradise Transformed* published
Geoff Hamilton dies

1997
Ground Force first broadcast

2000
Millennium Seed Bank Project at Kew opens to collect and conserve 10 per cent of the world's seed-bearing flora, (over 24,000 species) by 2010

Opposite: That's the thing
about Ivan Hicks's gardens –
you never know what to
expect.

First draft of the human genome
project
Birth of Dolly the sheep marks
the first mammalian cloning

2001
Twin Towers of the World Trade
Centre are destroyed by terrorists
Lindley Library goes high tech

2002
'Gardening in the Global
Greenhouse: The Impacts of
Climate Change on Gardens in
the UK' commissioned by the
National Trust, the Royal
Horticultural Society and others

2003
Monty Don takes over from Alan
Titchmarsh as the *Gardeners'
World* frontman

2004
The Great Pavilion appears at
Chelsea

Sophisticated outdoor electrical systems have
opened up a wealth of 'capabilities', as Mr
Brown might have said. Coloured uplighters
and fairy lights give trees a night-time
dimension. Fibre optics make sparkling effects
in a gravel garden by James Alexander-Sinclair.
Mood-altering images are projected in one of
Paul Cooper's gardens. Fog and mist machines
were used in Judy Toll's 'Puffing Mosses'
exhibit at the Stockholm Rosendal garden
show. Electric pumps have made fountains and
water spouts available to every small garden.
Electric-powered music, birdsong and tricks
do in a small space what hydraulics did in
seventeenth- and eighteenth-century
landscapes. One contemporary version of the
water trick squirts jets randomly along a
garden path – to the delight of the household's
children. The feature is part of a private
London garden by Christopher Bradley-Hole.

The Practitioners

Just as the materials and technologies
have changed, so too have the skills of
garden makers. Only some of them are
horticulturalists. Others are architects,
landscape architects, artists or poets.

David Hicks was an interior designer, who
moved his skills outside in the 1980s before
his death in 1998. He was committed to big,
bold structure and a colourful reinvention of
eighteenth-century 'borrowed views'. 'Come
back next summer,' he told me once. 'I will
have painted the landscape.' So he had – by
planting acres of purple flax in the fields
surrounding his Oxfordshire garden.

His namesake Ivan Hicks, the British garden
surrealist, has been at work since the 1960s.
At West Dean in Sussex he made a surreal
garden, sadly now destroyed, linked to
Magritte through the art patron Edward
James, who employed Hicks as his gardener
and flew him to Mexico and the south of
France to export his surreal garden designs
there. Hicks mingles sky-painted canvas
(a reference to Magritte); springs, to represent
the season of spring; mounts; ziggurat-shaped
foxglove trees; typewriters growing
sempervivum; and a wealth of sculpted 'found'
materials. Groombridge Place in Kent has
extended its gardens with some of Hicks's
more commercial work, and his designs have
been published in books, magazines and
television programmes since the 1980s.
For the last few years he has been working on
a private garden in Dorset, which includes a
conservatory Eden complete with serpent-like
path, a massive butterfly garden and law
books arranged to attract bookworms. Dig the
symbolism out of that lot, if you can.

Opposite: Albrecht Dürer appears to have monogrammed the turf at Ian Hamilton Finlay's brilliant garden at Little Sparta in Lancashire.

There are important gardens today in which symbolism plays as much a part as the plants, in a tradition reinvented by the poet Ian Hamilton Finlay at his garden in the Scottish borders. He uses landscape as a canvas for jokes, philosophies and classical and cultural references. The German artist Albrecht Dürer has 'signed' part of the landscape, Little Sparta, which was first carved out of a windswept moor in the 1960s. Since then, Hamilton Finlay has made pools, grass hedges, Latin puns, blackcurrant hedges and various features riven with symbolism, which requires visitors to be as well read as their eighteenth-century ancestors. It is a physically remote garden, but Hamilton Finlay's work has found a wider audience in and outside international galleries. One of his poems, carved in stone and set into the ground, is on view around the Serpentine Gallery in Hyde Park.

Today the USA is an increasingly important source of radical garden design. The landscape architect Martha Schwartz, for instance, made her infamous bagel garden in 1979. It was a joke – a crazy installation to amuse her husband. The box-edged parterre infilled with purple gravel and varnished bagels appeared in Schwartz's front garden in a fashionable area of Boston, and became an icon of a new approach. Work by her fellow countrymen

George Hargreaves (landscaper at the 2000 Sydney Olympics) and Topher Delany are widely published and discussed in Britain and elsewhere.

Another American, the architect Charles Jencks, and his English wife, the late Maggie Keswick (an authority on Chinese gardens), made a breathtakingly beautiful earthwork landscape in the Scottish borders. Called the Garden of Cosmic Speculation, its sensuous curves and folds are based on mathematics, Chinese landscape theory and quantum physics. It has echoes of many other great landscapes: eighteenth-century Claremont and Studley Royal; Percy Cane's mid twentieth-century grass terraces at Dartington Hall, Devon; the grass amphitheatre at Denmark's University of Aarhus, and Janis Hall's 1980s' undulating turf 'Waterland' in Connecticut. The Keswick/Jencks landscape is dramatic, and its use of plants is instructive. After two centuries of plant wealth – some might say confusion – the Garden of Cosmic Speculation uses only a few well-chosen trees and shrubs. And a lot of grass.

Tony Heywood is also keen on grass – he turfed a London gallery which exhibited his garden installations in 1999. Heywood, an artist/gardener, became the Church

Commissioners' head gardener in 1984, and began by experimenting with some awkward spaces outside tower blocks around the Edgware Road in London. He uses wire wool, glass, plastic, rock, mist, pebbles, unusual lighting and even a few plants to make gardens that look good both from ground level and from sixteen storeys up. These high-specification structures, designed to withstand life in the public arena, are the alter ego of another late-twentieth-century development – Chris Parsons' dew gardens. In the 1990s, Parsons began tracing exquisite patterns in the early morning dew to make some of the most ephemeral gardens known.

Above: Charles Jencks' and Maggie Keswick's masterpiece, the Garden of Cosmic Speculation, uses bold earthworks just as Percy Cane did at Dartington Hall, Devon (above).

Hal Moggridge, the landscape architect who continues Brenda Colvin's practice, landscaped the National Botanic Garden of Wales (built in part with £22 million from the Millennium Commission). His broad walk there is bordered by herbaceous plantings and divided by a rill that replicates the curves of the nearby river and displays boulders arranged as a geological journey through time. At its zenith, Norman Foster's glass dome undulates with the surrounding hills. Further west, at the Eden Project in Cornwall, the landscape architect and historian Dominic Cole (the *Gardens Through Time* designer) created the landscape that cradles Nicholas Grimshaw's extraordinary geodesic domes.

The increasingly sculptural form of

fashionable landscapes and gardens – such as Heywood's work, the Eden Project and the Garden of Cosmic Speculation – is matched by the increasingly successful use of sculpture in gardens. Sculpture has had a chequered history in British gardens over the last two hundred years. Sometimes it has materialized as trophy collections of antiquities, sometimes as dismal reminders of dead pooches. Since the time of Barbara Hepworth and Henry Moore, however, sculptors and garden makers have worked together to integrate the art forms. The RHS's current president, Sir Richard Carew Pole, has installed a bronze, cone-shaped water feature beside a yew cone at Antony, his eighteenth-century Cornish home. He commissioned the piece in 1996 from William Pye, who has made garden

sculptures for the Prince of Wales and the former foreign secretary Lord Carrington. In Gloucestershire the biennial Quennington sculpture festival includes an unusual water sculpture in the river that runs through the garden at Quennington Old Rectory, Cirencester.

Garden design has rarely been so exciting and challenging, so discussed and debated – and so controversial. Plant lovers reckon that many of the new gardens aren't gardens at all because they have so much hard landscaping and so few plants. Meanwhile, those interested in the garden as a piece of sculpture or form are impatient with Britain's continuing plant obsession. This creative tension between flowers and formality is a familiar theme in

Britain and may explain our enduring love affair with the Arts and Crafts garden as perfected by Lutyens and Jekyll, and its graceful compromise between the two opposing sides. Whatever the reason, it is a garden style that continues to be made and enjoyed by many, and it is often referred to as the quintessential English garden.

Propagation

The tidal wave of new design ideas spread via the media. Even gardening tips went wild and one television programme suggested detonating dynamite under a manure heap to avoid troublesome barrowing and forking.

The designers Guy Cooper and Gordon Taylor's book *Paradise Transformed,* and their

Above: The 2001 Quennington Sculpture Festival included this water sculpture 'Millrace' by Simon Allison.

BBC2 series *The Curious Gardeners*, unearthed some remarkable designs, including the Garden of Cosmic Speculation, and stoked the fires of debate about the garden in the twenty-first century. Their own designs include a courtyard where a single water jet rises from a glass brick tank; the design of which echoes the trellis above and the owners' modern house. The garden historian Jane Brown's books focused attention on the importance of the Modern movement in gardens.

Garden magazines multiply – Britain now has over thirty dedicated magazines, including *Gardens Illustrated*, which was launched in 1993 and became the first British gardening journal to concentrate successfully on design. Then there is a spectrum of non-specialist magazines with gardening sections – *Country Life* is an obvious example. Newspaper garden sections also flourish. All of them address design and innovation, as well as the horticulture that had been the staple of garden columns since coverage began. When I took over *The Times* Weekend section, in 1991, a gardening column appeared only when pagination allowed. I installed two regular garden columnists, Stephen Anderton and George Plumptre, and by the time I left five years later, the weekly coverage ran to two or three pages, if not more. The *Daily Telegraph*

Opposite: Cooper and Taylor's glass fountain tank echoes the trellis in this London courtyard. Their book Paradise Transformed *germinated a new debate about the future of gardens and landscaping.*

Right: The BBC's Ground Force, *with Charlie Dimmock, Alan Titchmarsh and Tommy Walsh, outraged traditionalists with its instant garden makeovers, but the series helped to create a new generation of gardeners.*

produced a garden magazine supplement in the early 1990s and now runs a dedicated garden section, and many of the Sunday and middle-market Saturday garden sections now appear in glossy colour. Peter Seabrook's column in the *Sun* has run for decades, and the newspaper market in general commands healthy revenue from gardening advertisements.

The BBC continues to dominate garden broadcasting. *Gardeners' World* alone regularly reaches an audience of between four and five million viewers. After a brief sortie into garden visits and radical design, the programme returned to its horticultural roots as instructed by the appropriately named then controller of BBC2, Jane Root. In 2003 Alan Titchmarsh's long and successful stint at its helm came to an end and Monty Don took over. Meanwhile, one of the BBC's new presenters, Chris Beardshaw, was airborne. Using a helicopter to examine local landscapes, he helped garden owners to use

plants appropriate to their gardens. This planting theme has been growing since the 1980s, and became a focus at the 2003 Chelsea Flower Show, when several garden designs used native plants as their theme. It helped that International Biodiversity Day coincided with the show.

In 1997 Alan Titchmarsh launched the first of many makeover series. This one was called *Ground Force*. Each programme worked as follows: members of the public contacted the BBC explaining why they thought their child, parent, friend or spouse deserved to have their garden 'done'. The chosen garden was then transformed by Titchmarsh, Tommy Walsh and gardening's first female sex symbol, Charlie Dimmock. They constructed the new garden in days. If anybody other than Titchmarsh had fronted *Ground Force*, it would have flopped, but he was the nation's trusted gardener, and if he could 'do' a garden in days, then 'instant' gardening was OK. Viewing figures went through the roof. Nevertheless, television garden design was still relatively conservative.

Then along came Diarmuid Gavin. In BBC2's *Home Front in the Garden* he played games with scale, concrete, rusted metal, light, sound and even a drinks cabinet to transform otherwise ordinary suburban gardens into extraordinary places. He made terraces into jungles, and humdrum lawn rectangles into visual challenges. What's more, the garden owners paid for Gavin's makeovers.

Even one of gardening's elder statesmen, Sir Peter Smithers, an eminent plantsman for most of the twentieth century and into this one (he started young and was born in 1913), has helped to make horticulture cool. His digital photographs of his exquisite tree peonies and lilies have launched Diesel's international fashion range in New York, and Sir Peter is now working on a major book of flower photography destined for international publication.

The message was clear: gardening could be glamorous – and garden owners didn't have to spend years tilling the soil to make these new outside rooms. Professionals began to sign up to this new enthusiasm. The designer Paul Cooper, who scandalized Chelsea with an 'erotic' plot, reflects this need and makes instant gardens for his clients by prefabricating everything off site. And specialist nurseries now supply an increasing number of large specimens – including massive *Magnolia grandiflora* and topiarized yew to create instantly 'mature' gardens.

Today the BBC is exploring a new theme – the spiritual side of gardens. The 2003 series called *The Plantsman* looked at arranging plants according to their emotional meaning to the garden owner. The programme was dreamt up by the BBC's Owen Gay and others appointed to cultivate an annual crop of new ideas for garden broadcasting. This one touched on the plants that remind us of friends and lovers, or of holidays and other special events.

Watching Gardens Grow

Small-screen gardening has flourished into a source of inspiration and instruction to millions of gardeners. Garden visiting has a similar role, having grown from a minority eighteenth-century hobby to today's massive pastime.

The National Gardens Scheme (NGS) made gardens more accessible in 1927 by persuading 607 private gardens to open to the

public to raise money for charitable causes. Eventually, the gardens' opening times and descriptions were published in the NGS's annual 'yellow book', which became a bible for any keen gardener. In 1970 1,224 gardens opened through the yellow book and raised £52,000 for charity. By 1987 they had raised £600,000 through a hugely increased gardens list, including one or two National Trust landscapes and some exquisite private gardens. These include Westwell Manor in Oxfordshire, an opulent, beautiful late twentieth-century variation on the garden 'rooms' theme, which opens only once a year. Today over 3,500 gardens open for the NGS, which gives over £1 million a year to the Gardeners' Benevolent Fund and other charities.

Then there are commercial guides. *The Shell Gardens Book* appeared in 1964, with the news that between one and two million people a year visited gardens. In the 1980s Graham Rose, garden correspondent of the *Sunday Times*, and Peter King began the *Good Gardens Guide*, which has become a treasured annual on the garden scene. Today King estimates that today about thirty million people pay to visit parks and gardens in Britain every year. The latest addition to the library of annual garden guides is the *RHS Garden Finder*, edited by Charles Quest-Ritson.

Garden visiting was given a new impetus by the restoration of the nineteenth-century Heligan Gardens in Cornwall and the

meticulous archaeological work at William III's Privy Garden at Hampton Court, which now looks as it would have in 1702. Tim Smit, one of the driving forces behind the work at Heligan (he is also one of those behind the Eden Project), speaks passionately about taking gardens out of aspic, whatever their age: 'If you can't make love in a garden, or get drunk in it, for God's sake tarmac it over.' Leaving aside the fact that recent legislation makes it illegal to make love in a garden, Smit's sentiment seems embodied at Heligan, which is one of the most visited gardens in the country, despite being off the beaten track. It popularized restoration work independent of the National Trust. Painswick Rococo Garden in Gloucestershire and eighteenth-century

Painshill in Surrey, both restored by private trusts, had led the way in the 1980s, but Heligan used television as its chief publicity tool to great effect and made restoration projects appear accessible – and fun. Heligan keeps interest high by running as a 'living' historic garden where visitors can watch gardeners using nineteenth-century techniques – lethal chemical regimes aside. Heritage Lottery Fund grants help fuel the restoration craze, although some still have to raise money independently. Seventeenth-century Aberglasney near Carmarthen is the most recent major restoration. In 2002 the BBC began its first garden restoration series, which, as always, sent garden visiting numbers sky high.

Above: The Ravine came in the later restoration phases at Heligan, having begun life in the early twentieth century as an echo of the Alps. Then it became a fernery before being overwhelmed by Cornwall's fecundity.

Shows and Public Parks

Far more is expected of gardens than a good display of plants, which is why garden shows, as well as flower shows, are thriving. During the twentieth century flower shows adhered mostly to the strict horticultural criteria set by the RHS, whose rules are observed by many independent village and county shows. The new garden shows have no such inhibitions.

France's Chaumont-sur-Loire international garden festival was launched in 1991, and in the years that followed showcased some of the West's most extraordinary designs. There was a garden of plastic phalluses that rose and fell out of the earth, as well as more attractive plots, such as a garden of woven willows, and a high wall of moss, ferns and other moisture-loving plants kept fed and watered by nutrient-rich water from a leaky pipe at the top of the installation. It was by Patrick Blanc, who has gone on to make vertical gardening chic: at the Pershing Hall hotel in Paris he has created a monumental wall garden with three hundred plant varieties clustered lushly together. Recently Chaumont-sur-Loire introduced an annual theme, including 'Eroticism' and, in 2003, 'Weeds'. In 2002 the UK began its own version of this show at Westonbirt Arboretum in Gloucestershire – it included a garden of brightly coloured fake flowers.

Opposite: Garden shows, but not as we know them. Chaumont-sur-Loire led the way with radical, sometimes outrageous, designs. In 2002 the UK came up with its own version of this festival at Westonbirt Arboretum (left).

The hunger for anything to do with gardens means that these new shows cohabit peacefully with Chelsea, which retains absolute pre-eminence socially, horticulturally and in the media. It remains a flower show and its show gardens remain traditional – with the occasional exception. In 1997 Christopher Bradley-Hole wowed Chelsea with a modernist garden. White and carmine concrete was softened by mauve alliums, purple iris and fennel, and punctuated by Latin quotations carved on to stone plaques. Bradley-Hole says he was

astonished that the garden was so well received – he had expected it to be 'hated'. The general mood that year was exhilarating – the millennium was close and people seemed eager to embrace new ideas.

That May Day, a couple of weeks before Chelsea, Tony Blair was voted in as prime minister, the first Labour leader since Margaret Thatcher defeated James Callaghan in 1979. He followed the ecological trend at 10 Downing Street by letting *Blue Peter* install a wildlife pond. London's newt-fancying mayor Ken Livingston was ahead of the game – he'd had a wildlife pond for years in his tiny west London garden, and surrounded it with native plants.

The Channel Tunnel has had an impact on garden design by bringing Paris within the realms of the British day trip – and RHS members now have free access to several gardens on mainland Europe. By the end of the century Paris had become a place of pilgrimage for anyone interested in park design. Gilles Clement and Alain Provost's Parc André Citroën was completed by 1992, and in the same decade Wirtz International, a family firm from Belgium, spun their twentieth-century designs across the Tuileries in Paris. Peter Wirtz also designed the Duchess of Northumberland's gardens at Alnwick, which are being built as I write – although parts, including the 120-jet random fountain system, are already working. Back in Paris the classically beautiful Bagatelle rose gardens in the Bois de Boulogne continue to attract admirers – and in 2000 they made an interesting contrast with a nearby gnome exhibition that appeared around the Trianon.

Big Business

Gardening is a growth industry in every sense. At the moment about twenty million Britons consider themselves active gardeners, so it was no surprise that investors queued up to put money into the garden dot-com companies that germinated at the end of the twentieth century. Crocus, the online garden centre, had a firmer foundation than most. Its founders, Mark Fane and his partners, bought the landscaping arm of Waterers, near London, which had housed a nursery since the late 1700s. Crocus launched from Waterers' old mail-order packing station in October 1999. Through a curious twist of history, the mail-order garden business, killed off by the 1971 postal strike and by garden centres, was revived by Internet shopping.

Only a few of the garden internet companies survived. Crocus is one of them, although its long-term selling power has yet to be proved. The RHS and BBC garden sites have evolved into well-presented information sources. Newspapers, too, include gardening on their

sites, either as an online reproduction of features and stories published in the paper, or as online question-and-answer sessions, like the one I write every Friday for *The Times*.

Research shows that some Internet users print out relevant garden pages – say on pruning – to take with them into the garden. Given that most sites are still accessed free of charge, it's cheaper and quicker than having to buy a book. So the Internet has been part of today's 'instant gardening' movement.

The Internet is also instrumental in greener garden maintenance because it is a swift and efficient source of biological controls. These controls are used against an increasing

Opposite: Christopher Bradley-Hole's cool, clean-lined 1997 garden at Chelsea.

Above: The courtyard gardens at Chelsea, like this Mondrian-style plot, reflects the ever-diminishing size of our gardens.

number of pests in and outside the green-house because the EU has effectively outlawed so many pesticides. Many herbicides have also been banned, and in some nurseries replaced by mini-tractors with sensor-controlled mini-hoes. All the same, the Scotts Company still manufactures many chemical controls and continues its search for garden chemicals without harmful side-effects.

Profits generated by gardening have encouraged some businesses to sponsor societies and clubs that might otherwise struggle. The Society of Garden Designers conferences are sponsored, and the Garden Writers Guild, set up in 1992, has attracted a wealth of sponsorship. Today it is a thriving society, with workshops, lectures, visits and an annual awards lunch at the Savoy.

The RHS in the Twenty-first Century

Large regional flower shows began to appear in the 1990s, bringing many of Chelsea's professional exhibitors to family-friendly showgrounds around the country. (Chelsea continues to be a no-go show for children.) Most of the new shows are run by the RHS and are evidence of a cultural change that can be traced back to its 1985 Review Committee report. This highlighted the need to give better service to members outside the south-east (an issue that had worried the society for over a century), and to find more sources of regular income to fund research programmes, libraries, gardens, the advisory service, free schools membership, bursaries and the Britain in Bloom campaign. The society decided that regional shows would benefit the existing membership and attract new members, thus increasing regular income.

The Malvern Spring Show was launched by the RHS in 1988. Five years later the show's policy was on a roll. The society helped to run the Harlow Carr show and to start News International's short-lived International Spring Gardening Fair. The fair may be best remembered for having been promoted by one of the *Sun*'s page three beauties, a petal on each nipple. The most successful event that year was the launch of the BBC's *Gardeners' World Live*, in which the RHS was closely involved. Finally, 1993 saw the society take over the Hampton Court Flower Show, which had started life three years earlier as Adrian Boyd & Partners' brainchild. Scotland's Garden Show, started by the RHS, came and went without catching on, but Tatton Park continues to grow each year. The new strategy was a success. Membership rose from its mid-1980s' level of 90,000 to about 320,000 in 2002.

Opposite: Alnwick Castle's cascade with hornbeam tunnels was commissioned by the Duchess of Northumberland and designed by Jacques Wirtz.

In accordance with other recommendations of the 1985 report, television companies were charged for Chelsea coverage, Chelsea's burgeoning visitor numbers were limited and the Lindley Library was rehoused – although not by moving the entire RHS headquarters to Wisley as first suggested. Another idea, put forward by Sir Simon Hornby in 1995, during his presidency, was that the Lindley Library alone should transfer to Wisley. Uproar ensued, followed by a vote of the membership – the first in the society's history – and a compromise. The main library would stay at the Vincent Square HQ, but move in 2001 to a purpose-built, atmosphere-controlled

area designed by Rick Mather. It was quite a change. Research work used to mean climbing the echoing stairs at Vincent Square (the lift seemed to take for ever) to attic rooms piled high with books. The head librarian, Brent Elliott, and his staff would bring book requests up from various mysterious rooms that were out of bounds to readers. Today the Lindley Library is hooked up to the Internet, the desks are set up for PC users, and Elliott and his staff operate a computerized catalogue. The Lindley Library is still open, free of charge, to anyone who cares to use it.

The increasingly high profile and growing

commercial success of the RHS attracted envy and criticism. Some claimed that the society was steamrollering regional distinctiveness, others that higher income came at the price of falling standards. The society's commercial success certainly presents a conundrum. Without funds from a growing membership, the society cannot pay for its charitable and educational work. To do so they have to maintain the 'virtuous circle' (in the current director-general Andrew Colquhoun's phrase) of money-making ventures (publishing, shows and so forth) to generate funds for the RHS, which is a charity. It doesn't please everyone, particularly those who feel that membership is now simply a matter of signing a cheque, rather than being recommended for membership and seconded, the RHS has abandoned its role as a learned society. This criticism is being addressed: the quarterly journal *The Plantsman* serves the more expert section of the membership.

Growing Fair Trade

On the international scene the RHS is trailblazing a scheme whereby gardeners of the future may be able to buy the plant equivalent of 'fair trade' chocolate. These fair trade plants may be awarded accreditation for benefiting their country of origin without destroying wild plant populations. For instance, cyclamen corms would be accredited if they had been propagated by a fairly paid local population in Turkey, rather than stripped from the wild.

The man behind this idea is Simon Thornton Wood, the RHS's Head of Science, Advice and Libraries. He is one of several people dealing with new attitudes to plant material that emerged at the end of the twentieth century. Many of these were expressed in a sort of botanical equivalent of copyright formulated at the 1992 Rio Earth Summit. World leaders at the summit agreed that profits from plants sold in one country have to be shared with the plants' country of origin. The agreement has consequences for Britain. Nurseries, usually low-margin businesses, do not have the resources to negotiate with a state in, say, Africa, let alone offer an acceptable deal that gives the country of origin some benefit. The RHS has a role as a negotiating link between the two parties so that nurseries can continue to offer new introductions to their customers. There is an issue beyond new plants, however, because we need a broader genetic base in order to breed cultivars able to withstand changes in climate and pest and disease populations – which is why it is in our interest to make the Rio Earth Summit agreements operate smoothly.

In essence the Rio Earth Summit agreement puts an end to what is now called 'plant plunder'. It is something of an irony that the label can be applied to one of the RHS's founders, Sir Joseph Banks, who introduced a wealth of plants from around the world. He was lauded for his work, and his introductions helped feed and fatten the emerging British Empire. Times and attitudes have changed, and today Britain, and many other nations, face pay-back time.

Carousel

If garden plant introductions have come full circle in the last couple of centuries, so too have public parks. By the mid twentieth century many of the glorious parks created in the nineteenth century were derelict, underfunded, unloved and often unrecognized as anything more than dog-walking grounds. In the nick of time the Heritage Lottery Fund (HLF) saw the need. To date it has ploughed £249 million into 371 parks. The money has been spent on everything from anonymous local green spaces to high-profile parks, including Battersea in London, where the riverfront has been rebuilt to Victorian plans that were never implemented. This has helped settle the 1985 Peace Pagoda into its surroundings. HLF money has also been used in the restoration of Joseph Paxton's remarkable Birkenhead Park, which helped inspire New York's Central Park.

There is a final circle now being completed in this history. This story began just as the landscape fashion was fading – now it has returned, and its sculptural shapes and forms are influencing many small gardens. There are some well-publicized examples: 'Capability' Brown's landscape at Heveningham Hall, in East Anglia has been completed (he died when only half the landscape had been installed), and Kim Wilke's late twentieth-century turf terraces link the house to the landscape. Then there are the two great Borders gardens, the Garden of Cosmic Speculation and Little Sparta, and the Eden Project in Cornwall. These monumental expressions of art join the growing vocabulary of disparate styles in outdoor design and gardens. A seemingly endless list of labels can be used to describe today's garden styles: symbolic, organic, modern, memorial, plant-orientated, ecological, genetic, sculptural, therapeutic, community, public, physic, productive, healing and erotic.

All this is perhaps best summed up by the poet, statesman and gardener Joseph Addison (1672–1719), who said, 'I think there are as many different kinds of gardening as poetry.'

8 Gardens Today

Designing in the Twenty-first Century

Opposite: My contemporary garden at RHS Harlow Carr was designed to reflect the hectic lifestyle of today's society, in which it is crucial to be able to use the garden both night and day.

Living with the evolving experiment that was the series *Gardens Through Time* was an interesting experience. I have always loved garden styles, both past and present, although I am not naturally a garden historian. Years ago, as a garden design student on a quest for something new, I did my very best to avoid references to traditional styles, indignant at the idea that they were, for the most part, the only accepted ones. However, on this series I began to confront the past and make an effort to understand it in a very practical way. It was a voyage of discovery that turned out to be an unexpected joy.

Right: A place to sit and reflect surrounded by plants isn't a modern invention – it was a popular feature of Regency gardens too.

Opposite: The Victorian passion for adventure meant that their gardens often had an exotic theme. In the RHS Harlow Carr garden we reflected this with the very popular Chinese theme.

The first thing I learnt is that very little is new. People have always shared a whole range of thoughts and feelings about innovation and tradition, and have always engaged in energetic debate with each other on the subject of gardens. Alongside those who simply love gardening there have been creators and explorers with huge egos, and still others fired by a desire to make money. Whatever the motivation, gardening has generally been underwritten by those with wealth, power and ambition, but that is far less true today.

Over the centuries, the passion for plants and creating gardens has not diminished: plant introductions, whether to a continent, a country or a garden, remain hugely exciting. While the tradition that we use our gardens for personal pleasure or simply to show off also remains unchanged, the status of the garden in society, and of the gardener who tends it, is now much more democratic. Media interest in gardening and increased freedom to travel have had a huge impact throughout the twentieth century, and this was the time, certainly in Britain, when the activity of gardening was opened up to the masses. As a result, gardening began to be reinterpreted to suit even the smallest spaces and budgets.

Followers of Fashion

During the course of the television series we featured many different styles of garden across the ages, and my reactions to them have surprised me. I discovered that the Regency period, for example, does very little for me; flower-beds cut into exotic shapes, plants put on 'pedestals' of soil raised out of lawns, and individual plants celebrated by standing them on their own, regardless of size, were conceits all too contrived for my liking. But maybe this is just the conditioning of my generation.

Sir Humphry Repton was a big name in Regency landscape design. He was a canny operator, who knew the market and was adept

Below: The Victorians really
pushed out the boundaries
on landscaping and
produced some eccentric
features – even by today's
standards – in their gardens.

these new garden owners. (Notably creating a craze for willow-hoop edged beds that were intended to look like flower-baskets delicately dropped around the lawn.) Of course, the owners of these middle-class gardens never got their hands dirty as we would today – they employed gardeners to do that for them.

Recreating the Regency garden at RHS Harlow Carr in Yorkshire for the series, using Repton's designs and the diktats of John Claudius Loudon's *Encyclopaedia of Gardening* (1822) as our sources and inspiration, was interesting, but the result was horribly twee. I had to remind myself that it was a style so new in its day that it would have been a revelation. Yet as I was creating these basket beds, the low-hooped guards that you still see around municipal lawns and flower-beds came to mind. All of a sudden, I was aware of their evolution and now I look at them with a fresh eye – I can see the progression from these basket beds to hanging baskets and accept that they probably had a similar genesis.

Victorian gardeners retained some of the styles of their forebears, but by comparison really pushed out the boundaries on colour, plant use and landscaping. Fun inspired the evolution of colour in their bedding out, while national obsessions with discovery and

at analysing and pleasing his clients, even developing new ways of presenting his plans to them – his illustrated 'red books' of plans became as sought after as his actual designs. At the same time, he was shrewd enough to recognize the shift that was occurring in the market-place. A brand new middle class was emerging, a new breed of professionals wielding power and influence. Their gardens weren't like the great estates of Milton Abbas or Blenheim; rather, they were smaller outdoor spaces which were attached to town houses and villas. Just as the gardening market has changed for us in the last ten or fifteen years, so it was subject to change then. Armed with this awareness, Repton distilled the big ideas to create a fashion that could be taken up by

adventure led to wonderfully absurd garden monuments, such as models of the Matterhorn. The virulence of contemporary debates between the likes of William Robinson, who idealized naturalized planting, and Sir Reginald Blomfield, who preferred more formal styles, was remarkable, and the different intellectual approaches must have been as stimulating then as they are today.

Through our 1920s' garden I came to understand and appreciate a later style that had plagued my youth as a design student – the herbaceous borders of Gertrude Jekyll. Only now do I find this style fascinating and appreciate how innovative it was at the time.

Working on the programme and reading the words of many great gardeners, I began to realize that if they were around today, they would still be the pioneers that they were in their own times. So what would Jekyll have been doing today? She would have been using her artist's eye, all right, but that eye wouldn't have been acquired from dabbling in watercolours, oils or needlework; today Jekyll would have moved on from the Impressionists and abstract artists to look at different elements of plants. Colour might still fascinate her, but is it sacrilegious to imagine that her present interest might be the subtle

greens of the exotic jungle look or an appreciation of how climate change has allowed to us to grow a wider range of plants and create a variety of moods? Or would she have indulged in garden installations? One thing is for sure: her radical artistic mind would not have remained static.

Of all the garden designers from previous centuries, Jekyll is the one whose legacy still relates most readily to what we do today. Her sense of plants, material, balance and proportion have had a profound influence on modern garden design. She perfected the herbaceous border, loved working with colour and, together with Edwin Lutyens, popularized the idea of a gardener working hand in hand with an architect to produce designs that perfectly balanced the effects of hard landscaping and planting. In fact, this is still an idea that needs further exploration. But, influential as it is, her style must not be idolized. The herbaceous border isn't something to be canonized; it is a totally contrived, albeit wonderful, vanity, but after a hundred years, should design not be moving on?

The 1950s' garden proved a disappointment to me. Despite the work of various excellent practitioners, no national appetite for gardening existed at that time for their ideas

to be welcomed. Today we live in acquisitive times, not unlike the Victorian era, but during the 1950s there just wasn't much money around; it was post-war, a time of rationing, and gardens weren't being commissioned. The country was changing radically, but this was mainly because people were trying to get back on their feet.

It's a big regret to me, brought home by wandering through the garden at Harlow Carr, that we didn't have great post-war innovators who stuck by their guns and created something new. Yes, a certain school did emerge, probably headed by Dame Sylvia Crowe, but it was quite elite and didn't impact massively on individual gardens. In other countries plenty was happening, but in Britain those creative types who could have brought something new to garden design were probably involved in architecture, furniture design or fashion: they certainly weren't working in gardens. I felt a certain sadness about the 1950s' plot at Harlow Carr, but my hope is that we can pick up the pieces and develop the new garden, the truly contemporary garden, from the ashes of what was started then.

The designs of the late 1960s and early 1970s were also disappointing to me, again partly as a result of our garden at Harlow Carr. The signature of this period is planting – acres of planting – through gravel. This leaves me cold. Yes, it does a job that people want: it produces an easy-maintenance area, but who wants purely easy maintenance in the real, trend-setting garden?

Walking through the decades from the 1920s' to the 1970s' garden, I couldn't help but feel that something had been lost along the way. The passion of the plant hunters, the excitement of new introductions, the use of plants in interesting ways were just, well, gone. Plants were included merely as architectural features or green fluff on the ground, intended to grow vertically or sometimes into each other and work in the background. The picture was completed by a fantasy lifestyle of happy kids playing volleyball around beautiful pools and chic furniture while the parents tended smouldering barbecues. But it was these very things that had excited me when, as a student, I devoured *The Small Garden* (1977) by John Brookes. Maybe I loved it because it was radically different from the traditional styles I was trying to escape from, and sometimes you need somebody who is doing things differently to lift you out of a rut. Inevitably, age and experience make you view things

Opposite: The reconstructed Jekyll and Lutyens garden at RHS Harlow Carr reflects the pair's trademark design features.

Above: Sadly, a lack of great contemporary innovators in garden design during the 1950s meant that our post-war garden at RHS Harlow Carr was as disappointing as the original gardens it represented.

Below and right: Our
Outdoor Room garden at
RHS Harlow Carr echoes
the obsession of garden
designers of the late 1960s
and early 1970s. Their style
relied heavily on plants
being used as architectural
features, often set against
a sea of gravel.

The Changing Face of Gardening

With all this inspiration and debate in mind, creating the final, present-day garden in the series of seven at RHS Harlow Carr was quite a daunting task. It's hard to summarize a continually changing time in gardening and garden design, especially as I have such a distinct and much debated take on the subject. I love creating gardens; it's what I've wanted to do since I was a child, and it continues to be a source of amazement and joy that I get to work on so many diverse projects in many different countries. I love being outdoors. I love the countryside. I love plants. I have always been fascinated by design in all its forms, and what I wanted to create in Yorkshire was something that was really relevant to the ideas and culture of the era in which I live, something contemporary.

with a much more critical eye, so perhaps that accounts for my change of heart. However, certain plants will forever be associated with this period. Just as *Acer palmatum dissectum* and bamboo spell out Japanese, so the sumach, the castor oil plant and the ground-cover rubus send me reeling back to a period between the 1950s and 1980s. Maybe it was great at the time but, luckily, we found gardening again and began to match it up with a true outdoor lifestyle.

I have always been against maintaining a status quo in the design world – fitting in and toeing the line and accepting the wisdom of the day whether you agree with it or not. From my earliest days as a designer I have wanted to use new plants – or plants that I thought of as new – such as big, exotic tree ferns and hardy bananas, particularly as we have this magnificent mild climate which means that we can successfully grow things that many of our predecessors would have thought too tender to survive in Britain. My personal ambition is to try and find out, through my own work and that of others, what the new, modern garden is or what it could be, but in order for me to achieve this, it is important for me to reflect on the recent changes in our gardening culture.

It has always been said that we on these islands are nations of gardeners, but I'm not sure how true this has been. Thanks to our temperate climate, we can grow an enormous number of plants, and while gardening has been a fantastic hobby and a way of nurturing, demonstrating and showing off, it has also been a plaything of the wealthy, a hobby dominated by the elite – and a very conservative elite at that.

In the earliest days gardens were used to grow food crops and plants for herbal remedies, oils and perfumes. They went on to become calm places for spiritual reflection, or parks or hunting grounds. As we have seen, the rich and powerful have pioneered grand garden styles over the last two hundred years, often to show off and follow fashionable trends. Over the centuries introductions from across the globe have brought new forms and colour, exciting the nobility in their mansions and the middle classes in their villas. In fact, gardening through the ages is a microcosm of social history – an occupation directed by people with money but carried out by the labouring classes.

Society has changed, of course, and wealth is distributed slightly more evenly now. Today there is a huge degree of home ownership, and families like to live in houses with gardens. As a result, there are more gardens than ever before, although they are probably now smaller than before, too. There's more money around and people have more leisure time, so they have become fascinated with design, quality and luxury. Lifestyles are geared towards the individual and emphasize consumer consumption – the clothes, the cars, the furniture and the hobbies that people reckon suit them. It is no longer one size or one style fits all. Design and fashion have invaded every area of life and become disposable – in our grandparents' day people lived with a particular style for a generation, now people reassess their look every four or five years.

Gardening was relatively slow to succumb to this fast-track change, as the population at large had for a long time inherited garden styles without question. The accepted tradition was for a couple to meet, marry, acquire a house and look to parents or grandparents for advice on how to cultivate the garden. A diet of traditional horticultural magazines and television programmes, such as *Gardeners' World*, have provided a gentle education, taking people in hand and showing them how to create beautiful middle-class gardens with flowers, fruit, compost heap and pathways, and how to update rockeries, hanging baskets, trellis and tubs on an annual basis. Having a garden was about digging, spraying roses, lifting dahlias and composting.

Today the term 'gardening' has broken away from being something that everybody understands and now means different things to different people. In recent years it has been opened up to everyone, and is now as much a part of popular culture as anything else you can think of. Of course, there remains an elite element and a certain snobbishness; to some it will always be a pursuit based on huge herbaceous borders and subtle colour palettes. For many, however, gardening has moved on from John Brookes's original premise of the room outside and is now about wanting an external space to reflect their personalities; it's something to be purchased, a lifestyle accessory that suits the owner, keeps maintenance to a minimum and maximizes enjoyment.

At the time of writing there's a general state of euphoria regarding the possibilities. People dream of having an urban paradise, but as these newly landscaped plots settle, the realities of what the more traditional gardener has always known will come to the fore. Gardens aren't just for seasonal use. If they are to be in any way exciting and rewarding, they need to be understood, nurtured and developed all year round.

I think the integrity and genuine interest in gardening will successfully develop long after the excitement of the new style has passed. The reason for this is simple: the nurturing of plants is seductive, and the magic and delight of growing something in a pot or the ground will, over time, seduce even the most cynical. People want their gardens to succeed, and the joy of looking after them will develop as horticultural pride evolves. A potted melianthus that I gave my sister-in-law has illustrated this very clearly for me. It has accompanied her on house moves, and every time I visit I am dragged into the garden to share her delight in something that, even in the middle of the winter, has turned out to be a dramatic specimen. To my astonishment and jealousy (because mine collapsed), her plant is flowering in December and January. So people who buy into the whole notion of creating a garden because they have seen Charlie Dimmock on television or have bought glossy

gardening magazines suddenly find themselves intensely proud of their achievements and want to know more. They start reading up about their plants and very soon discover their true likes and dislikes.

So what is this new gardener looking for? Let's start with the gloss. They want a particular style, but they want their own interpretation of it, and in some cases this means employing a specialist to do that for them. While garden designers and landscape contractors have always existed (remember Humphry Repton, Capability Brown, Gertrude Jekyll, *et al*), in the last ten years they have been especially welcomed by the middle classes, who are spending big money on creating gardens – sometimes as much as building an extension to the house. The client's brief now doesn't just involve beautiful plants, such as roses, delphiniums and dicksonias: features are also required, including decks, water, furniture and outdoor heaters. The market has responded to these demands and jumped at the chance to supply never-ending ranges of ephemera, from traditional to sleek and shiny.

The possibilities for gardens have expanded in people's minds, especially now that a green oasis is promoted as the antidote to a hectic lifestyle. The garden continues to be seen as a

peaceful paradise, but now we are allowed to add more functions. The cult of the shed as a masculine haven has led to a desire for garden rooms and pavilions, comfortable places to relax in or to work from. Meanwhile, barbecuing and dining outdoors have become de rigueur. All these functions, little more than pipe-dreams in previous decades, have now become essentials.

What these changes signify to me is that people have relaxed. Barriers have been broken down and possibilities have been opened up. There is a new feeling that we can do whatever we want in the garden, that we can express ourselves as we like and that it is not only residents of California who can have an outdoor lifestyle. We can be as wacky, as formal, as artistic or sedate as we want to be.

Above: Today's garden owners want more than just beautiful plants in their plots; gardens are now an extension of the home and need to be practical and entertaining spaces, and to be furnished accordingly.

Above: The outdoor room is even more relevant in garden design terms today, and my garden at RHS Harlow Carr moves the summerhouse idea on further with the addition of lighting and modern technological features.

We possess information on lots of different garden styles. We are beginning to realize where they came from, why they evolved and how appropriate they may be for us, which gives us the confidence to create an outdoor space tailored to our specific needs. We are not scared of gardens or slaves to them; their job is to work for us. We control the space, we decide what to install and when.

In time, when we get past the current phase of greedily acquiring the latest garden fashions, I am sure our decisions will become more intelligent and lead to fantastic developments. In Britain, thanks to the Royal Horticultural Society – which has nurtured the craft and science of gardening and provided forums for people to display their successes, and whose bicentenary *Gardens Through Time* celebrates –

we can draw on the rich legacy of passionate gardeners from previous generations.

Reflecting the Twenty-first Century

As you can imagine, designing a garden at Harlow Carr to encompass all the elements of twenty-first century living was very difficult, even though I had the advantage of creating the only plot that wasn't a pastiche or a mixture of styles from a particular period. I was able to determine the size of my plot and invent a contemporary scenario for its use. It was to be a 'normal' plot for a fictitious, design-conscious urban family who probably had a few children. This was also the disadvantage. As a garden designer, your best work will always be a collaboration with the client; it will evolve from the initial brief and the feedback on the proposed design. It will not be like other gardens you have created because everybody is unique and has a different sense of what they want and would like to achieve. Having no client as such at Harlow Carr took away this interaction, so I procrastinated endlessly until the very last moment. As a result, I'll never be fully happy with the design; as soon as I delivered it, I regretted it. Under the circumstances this was probably inevitable – a garden without people, without clients, will doubtless be static and lifeless. It becomes merely a display.

My prolonged procrastination also led to the garden being built in just three weeks at the end of the year. Unlike the other plots, we didn't get a chance to live with it, to see it develop over time or be planted in different seasons. However, a garden was created to reflect garden design in 2004, and whether it succeeds or fails is open to interpretation. It is an individual piece of work created in my individual style: I'm not suggesting that other people are creating gardens in exactly the same way, but the current obsessions, I hope, are summed up in it.

For my modern garden I wanted to reflect the features that we typically find in a new house today, so I clad the boundaries of the plot in concrete walls against a façade that imitates the back of the ground floor of a semi-detached urban dwelling. Within this I placed a very strong shape – an oval wooden wall on a metal frame that was open at its main sides. A circular opening leads from the practical patio area, which could house dustbins and washing-line. Walking through this 'moon gate', the visitor arrives in the main ornamental garden, which consists of borders to the side, a small lawn and steps that lead down to an integrated garden pavilion with a small courtyard to the rear. The overall design was contrived to make the best use of the space. The shape and flow of the garden are all inherently sculptural. The hidden bits (around the back of the pavilion) allow children to create dens, or could even be used for a compost heap or small garden shed.

The steel frame was partially clad using one of my favourite materials, western red cedar, a beautiful timber that has a luxurious feel to it and reflects our new-found interest in natural textures. The outer rendered wall was painted an aubergine colour, which helped to highlight and provide contrast for the planting. This was done to show that raw concrete walls in a garden need not be a source of despair; they can be easily aged with planting or transformed by colour. Be warned, though, that getting the colour right when hard-landscaping gardens is an art that, generally speaking, we have yet to master.

The planting in my 2004 garden was designed to reflect our new horticultural enthusiasm. Today people want a little bit of everything. I therefore included native trees, such as birch, some cottage garden planting that Gertrude Jekyll would be proud of, some so-called new exotics, such as dicksonias, which the Victorians revelled in before we rediscovered them as style accessories, and plants that are special to me, such as *Solanum crispum*

'Glasnevin', a variety selected and cultivated at my old alma mater, the National Botanic Gardens, Glasnevin, in Dublin. A specimen tree, *Catalpa bignonioides*, was planted in the lawn because I admire its luxurious foliage and the shape it takes on as it matures. In time, it will link all the other elements together. The birch trees outside the frame were used to create a link with the surrounding landscape, to borrow from existing woodland and make the garden appear to be part of that.

Melding Past with Present

An interesting element of this project was to explore the styles of the six other periods chosen to celebrate the bicentenary of the Royal Horticultural Society, and through them to be conscious of the continual development of the garden and the changing design and techniques that they revealed. To this end, I tried to incorporate elements of what I had learnt throughout the series and echo some of the key features of these designs wherever they were relevant to my modern approach.

The idea of creating a garden to show off to our peers has been with us since Repton's time, but is now achieved in different ways. For example, although my catalpa stands proudly in a lawn, it is not raised on a soil platform as it would have been in Regency style. In the modern context its shape is appreciated as part of the overall structure of the garden. Another departure from the past is that I don't have any nasty man-traps to capture marauding thieves because my specimens are not worth what they would have been in Repton's day!

Have I drawn on Victorian eccentricity? Well, perhaps the fibre optics are a modern equivalent, their night-time twinkling providing the same fascination as a reconstructed Matterhorn. I don't pretend to be naturalistic in style like Robinson, and I certainly don't go for the formality of Blomfield, but I enjoy the fact that they had their arguments and I certainly have mine.

Later eras have also contributed to my garden. Jekyll and Lutyens fill me with admiration for the way that different minds and different disciplines can work together, each respecting what the other does. There is no snobbery of the designer versus the plants person, but a harmony that I hope my garden sums up. Even trends from the 1950s to the 1970s played their part. They gave me an appreciation of structure and materials, which I tried to use more sympathetically. They also made me realize that sometimes less is more, influenced me to take into account low-

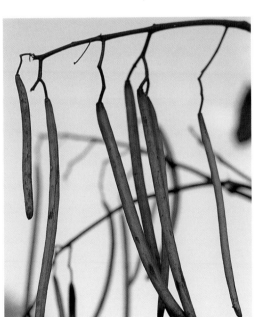

Left: In my 2004 garden at RHS Harlow Carr I tried to reflect the other period gardens in my planting scheme, using old favourites alongside more modern ones. Although dicksonias and phormiums appear to be a modern fashion, they have actually been around since Victorian times.

maintenance aspirations and embodied the idea of gardens being inspired by structures, sculptures and art. My aim was to do all this with a lot more coherence.

Designing the garden at Harlow Carr made me sympathize with all the other gardeners whose work has inspired us over the past two hundred years because, like them, I'd probably be none too pleased to see a bastardized version of my work totally out of context.

When I create gardens they are always for real clients, and are inspired by the site, the aspect or something said. In an ideal world, I wouldn't have put my garden behind high walls beside a busy road; instead, I would have tried to fit it in with the landscape of Harlow Carr.

The real test of my garden is to imagine living there. Just make believe for a while that it's a place for you and your family to enjoy. What are the good points? It works as a unit, it's concise and it contains an interesting selection of plants from different periods, mainly over the last two hundred years. It would be an easy garden to maintain and yet it has elements of the great British gardening tradition: a summerhouse, a lawn that acts as a soothing rug, and a thoughtful collection of plants – some used as specimens, others to link the garden with the local scenery. It's a garden that will always look well, that has its maintenance areas (wormery, compost heap, rotting log heap) hidden away, and that will let you actually garden. It is also a fun place for children to make forts and dens away from the prying eyes of adults. Last, but not least, it embraces technology, having a robotic mower to cut the grass, plus fibre optics and neon as entertainment lighting.

The experiences at Harlow Carr were, to me, at least partly about the enjoyment of nostalgia, especially when working with George Dunnington, a former public gardener of many years experience. He regaled me with stories and told me about his meeting Sylvia Crowe. (He also recalled the amusement of workers at a power station where she designed a garden known affectionately as 'Dame Sylvia's breasts'. These were two cone-shaped mounds full of power station debris and planted in an extraordinary way.) What also intrigued me about George, who was on site all the time we were making the gardens and acted as tour guide to official visitors, was his enthusiasm for innovation. Far from being attached to the grand Edwardian-style bedding schemes that he had created for councils, he thought it was great to see things moving on, and remarked on some visitors' reticence to accept anything new. It was so refreshing to see the true spirit of gardening manifest itself through George, to witness his delight at being involved in the creation of a contemporary garden, and to observe him passing on all his knowledge and love of gardening through his grandnephew Ian, who also worked on the site.

It was a particular pleasure to work with Jane Owen, whose knowledge and enthusiasm were infectious. Some of the most special moments for me on *Gardens Through Time* were the lively debates between us. Indeed, the series was a fascinating experience for everyone who worked on it, illuminating ideas and crystallizing thoughts in ways that constantly took us by surprise. It showed that while design is constantly evolving, the fundamentals of gardening remain unchanged. We each do our own thing in our own way, just as previous generations of gardeners have done – and long may that continue.

Regency Garden 1804–37
RHS Garden Harlow Carr, Yorkshire

Regency gardens were all about informality and new plant discoveries, but mostly about the emerging middle classes showing off. In an era when the range of plant species was quite limited, gardens relied on other elements for the 'wow' factor. Our Regency Town House Garden at Harlow Carr includes many of these fashionable devices.

The 'best' lawns were those that were carefully cultivated, but broken up by meandering paths or island beds. As the style demands, our path leads the visitor past beds scattered with must-have plants towards surprise hidden features. Hazel branches hooped around the edge of these beds recreate Humphry Repton's much-copied idea of flower baskets daintily scattered around the lawn. Other beds pay homage to the contemporary fashion of planting a single specimen plant. Bizarre as it sounds, expensive and treasured plants were placed in an exposed bed surrounded only by bare soil. As suggested by Loudon, our *Cornus florida* is planted in this way and labelled with its botanical and common names and country

1 Decorative pineapples
2 Yorkstone paving
3 Auricula theatre
4 Gravel path
5 Holly hedge
6 Hornbeam hedge
7 Immaculate lawn and hazel hoop-edged beds
8 Thatched summerhouse
9 Seat around existing oak
10 Fruit garden

of origin written on a white-painted brick.

Halfway round the garden, the visitor is invited to sit in a rustic summerhouse – all then the rage. Traditionally made from larch and ash timber and topped with a thatched roof, the building has a textured feel inside too, created by a decorative panel and hazel patterns around the walls.

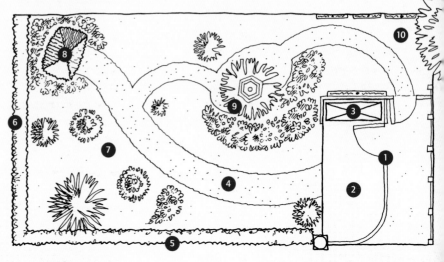

Tucked around the corner at the end of the garden is a tree seat. In an age of romance and passion, this provided a secluded meeting area or a place for reflection.

Left: Auriculas arrived at the end of the sixteenth century, but became stars of their own theatres during the Regency period. The black background highlighted the colour and delicacy of the the flowers, which appeared for only two or three weeks at a time. This was high fashion and showing off at its best.

PLANT LIST

The fruit garden

Redcurrant 'Laxton's Number One'
Vaccinium vitis-idaea
Whitecurrant 'White Grape'
Pink Currant 'Champagne'
Sambucus nigra
Raspberry 'Yellow Antwerp'
Gooseberry 'Keepsake'
White Currant 'White Versailles'
Wild Strawberry
Morello Cherry
Pear 'Louise Bonne of Jersey'
Pear 'Williams' Bon Chrétien'
Pear 'Catillac'

Round bed

Rosa 'Charles de Mills'
Rosa x *centifolia* 'De Meaux'
Rosa 'Petite de Hollande'
Platycodon grandiflorus
Polemonium caeruleum
Catanache caerulea
Dianthus carthusianorum
Centaurea dealbata
Lathyrus grandiflorus
Lathyrus odoratus 'Cupani'
Linum narbonense

Tadpole bed

Rosa 'Celsiana'
Rosa 'Marie Louise'
Rosa x *centifolia* 'Spong'
Rosa 'Violacea'
Dianthus 'Queen of Sheba'
Aquilegia vulgaris 'Nora Barlow'
Stokesia laevis
Knautia arvensis
Galega officinalis
Dianthus 'Paisley Gem'
Echinacea purpurea
Lunaria rediviva
Ranunculus acris 'Flore Pleno'
Catanache caerulea
Alcea rosea
Nigella damascena
Convolvulus tricolor
Reseda odorata
Salvia horminum
Consolida ajacis

Screen

Ligustrum lucidum
Prunus lusitanica
Prunus laurocerasus
Ilex aquifolium 'Ferox'
Euphorbia corallioides
Euonymus japonicus
Taxus baccata 'Fastigiata'
Viburnum tinus
Chaenomeles cathayensis
Kalmia latifolia

Summerhouse

Staphylea trifolia
Rhododendron campylocarpum
Daphne mezereum
Clethra alnifolia
Syringa vulgaris
Ilex aquifolium 'Bacciflava'
Cornus mas
Rhamnus cathartica
Ligustrum lucidum
Euonymus japonicus
Pyracantha coccinea
Ptelea trifoliata
Caragana arborescens
Cotinus coggygria
Syringa x *persica*
Viburnum tinus
Hydrangea quercifolia
Philadelphus coronarius
Ilex aquifolium 'Ferox Argentea'

Specimen shrubs

Hamamelis virginiana
Ilex aquifolium 'Argentea Marginata'
Cornus florida
Chionanthus virginicus
Spartium junceum
Rosa 'Chaplin's Pink Climber'
Wisteria sinensis
Camellia japonica 'Alba Plena'
Agave americana
Convolvulus cneorum
Agapanthus africanus
Fuchsia magellanica

Trees

Fraxinus excelsior 'Pendula'
Cercis siliquastrum

Herbaceous border

Lobelia siphilitica
Campanula persicifolia var. *alba*
Geum montanum
Digitalis lanata
Paeonia peregrina
Geranium sanguineum var. *striatum*
Lobelia cardinalis
Aconitum Anglicum Group
Ranunculus acris 'Flore Pleno'
Alcea rosea 'Nigra'
Salvia azurea
Campanula collina

Paeonia lactiflora
Astrantia major
Lychnis coronaria
Chamerion angustifolium 'Album'
Coreopsis lanceolata
Aquilegia vulgaris 'Nora Barlow'
Ranunculus montanus double
Calamintha cretica
Verbascum chaixii
Campanula alliariifolia
Astrantia maxima
Coreopsis verticillata
Paeonia mascula
Eryngium amethystinum
Plantago major 'Rosularis'
Lupinus arboreus
Lysimachia ephemerum
Galium verum
Lychnis flos-jovis
Nepeta sibirica
Digitalis ferruginea
Platycodon grandiflorus 'Albus'
Inula ensifolia
Silene dioica 'Flore Pleno'
Knautia arvensis
Geum rivale

Mid-Victorian Garden 1837–70
RHS Garden Harlow Carr, Yorkshire

Increased travel and wealth made the mid-Victorian era an exciting time for gardeners and designers. Plant hunter Robert Fortune's work triggered an interest in all things Chinese and, as a result, many gardens incorporated elements of this style – one of the most famous being at Biddulph Grange, Staffordshire. Both our pagoda and our gravel parterre that you see on entering the garden

fashionable plants of the time, such as the Douglas fir. Specimen plants were still the ultimate garden accessory, and the orecania or monkey puzzle tree was another popular import that was seen as a status symbol. In contrast to the Regency period, specimen plants would be colourfully underplanted, in order to draw the eye towards them.

Armed with these plant arrivals from across the world, and particularly from South America and South Africa, a new style of planting emerged – 'Italianate' bedding. Our scheme, re-created beneath a formal stone balustrade, follows the rules of a design based on geometric patterns in which each block contains one specific

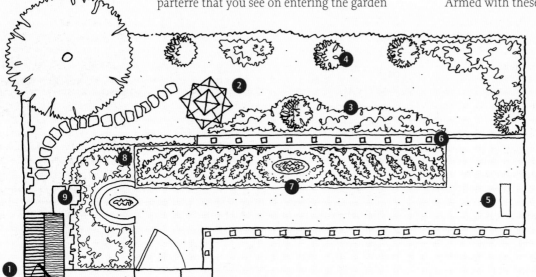

1 Potting shed
2 Pagoda
3 Evergreen shrubbery
4 Monkey puzzle tree
5 Seat
6 Reconstituted stone balustrade
7 Italianate bedding
8 Fernery
9 Pulhamite wall

were influenced by Biddulph and echoed its use of the most popular Chinese motif of the time – the dragon. To add to the Chinese feel, the space has been planted up with golden bamboo and purple hazel.

This garden leads into another popular style altogether, the shrubbery. Evergreen shrubberies provided privacy and all-year colour and allowed gardeners to use

colour. It is a very formal style that relied on brightly coloured annuals and foliage plants for maximum effect. At Harlow Carr we used pelargoniums (notably the Victorian favourite geranium 'Mrs Pollock' – loved for its vibrant foliage), lobelias, petunias and calceolerias.

Amongst the inventions of the age was one that reflected the Victorians' love of imitating and improving upon nature. Pulhamite was a

man-made substance that looked as natural and realistic as real stone, but was significantly cheaper, and which enabled gardeners to re-create walls or rockeries on which to display their collection of rock plants. Our Pulhamite wall needed a little work to create the right colour, but wasn't a bad attempt, particularly as we didn't have the benefit of the secret recipe for making the material. We planted the wall up with some Victorian favourites, such as little-leaf cotoneaster, box-leaf honeysuckle and the must-have plant of the period – Boston ivy.

No trendsetting mid-Victorian garden was complete without a fernery, so we dedicated the area between our Pulhamite wall and the formal bedding to ferns. The idea was to re-create the natural habitat for these plants but in typical Victorian excess – whole trees were used to create stumperies and mock ruins were often added. At Harlow Carr we created a smaller version of this style using birch logs and stones as a base for such popular plants as *Osmunda regalis* (a British native that did well everywhere) and other curling, dramatic ferns.

PLANT LIST

Left bed

Prunus lusitanica
Berberis darwinii
Aucuba japonica
Cistus x hybridus
Phillyrea angustifolia
Rhododendron 'Fastuosum Flore Pleno'
Rhododendron 'Nobleanum Venustum'
Ilex aquifolium
Choisya ternata
Phillyrea angustifolia
Ribes sanguineum
Daphne odora 'Aureomarginata'
Mahonia aquifolium

Right bed

Juniperus sabina 'Tamariscifolia'
Prunus laurocerasus
Lonicera fragrantissima
Ilex x altaclerensis 'Lawsoniana'
Phillyrea angustifolia
Ceanothus x veitchianus
Rhododendron 'Jacksonii'
Rhododendron 'Cunningham's White'
Rosa 'William Lobb'
Forsythia suspensa
Rhododendron 'John Waterer'
Mahonia japonica
Skimmia japonica
Garrya elliptica

Prunus lusitanica
Corylus maxima 'Purpurea'
Phyllostachys nigra
Ligustrum ovalifolium 'Aureum'

Shrubs for Pulhamite

Cytisus multiflorus
Santolina chamaecyparissus
Hedera helix
Parthenocissus tricuspidata
Juniperus squamata
Pinus mugo
Cotoneaster microphyllus
Hedera helix 'Cavendishii'
Lonicera nitida
Hypericum calycinum
Vinca minor
Cistus x purpureus

Trees

Pseudotsuga menziesii
Pinus sylvestris
Sequoia sempervirens
Salix 'Chrysocoma'
Araucaria araucana

Ferns

Asplenium scolopendrium
Athyrium filix-femina
Dryopteris filix-mas
Osmunda regalis
Matteuccia struthiopteris
Polystichum polyblepharum
Asplenium scolopendrium Crispum Group
Asplenium trichomanes

Blechnum spicant
Blechnum chilense
Cystopteris dickieana
Dryopteris affinis
Dryopteris dilatata
Gymnocarpium dryopteris
Onoclea sensibilis
Polystichum aculeatum
Polystichum 'Divisilobum Group'
Phegopteris connectilis
Polypodium vulgare

Above: Our garden included formal balustrades as well as a reconstructed potting shed for the gardeners. This was painted in the authentic Reckett's Crown Blue, which was a clothes-cleaning agent that also seemed to ward off flies. These sheds were immaculately kept, with tools neatly hung.

Late-Victorian Garden 1870–1901
RHS Garden Harlow Carr, Yorkshire

The Late Victorian era continued to celebrate the eccentric and the new. The middle classes were enjoying a new wealth and with more choices for planting and accessorizing, consumer society had begun.

The gardens of this time were an eclectic mix of features and styles, and often ended up as a hotch-potch of ideas. In our garden we incorporated many of these trends.

The most dramatic feature in our recreated garden, though, reflects the love of world adventure and the creative spirit of the age. The Matterhorn was first conquered by British explorer Sir Edmond Wymper in 1865 and was famously recreated on a major scale at Friar Park in Henley. Our version was substantially smaller, but even so managed to use 120 tons of local stone. This glorified

1 Cold conservatory
2 Lawns and carpet bedding
3 Matterhorn
4 Stepping stone path
5 Lawns
6 Children's garden
7 Vegetables
8 Sundial
9 Stone balls

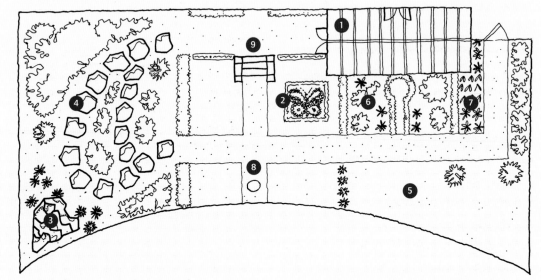

The invention of the automatic thermostat made heating a hot house reliable and easy, and, with glass becoming a cheaper material, conservatories became a must-have feature. The real excitement of these glasshouses lay in the exotic array of new plants you could grow in them. Such plants were laid out on benches as talking points with orchids being the ultimate accessory.

rock garden also provided an excellent way to display one of the many current planting fashions of the day – alpines. At the top of the formation we planted smaller flowering alpines such as *Phlox subulata* and anemonies, and around the base we scattered the popular low-growing, spreading conifers of the time, which were dwarf varieties of the larger pine tree.

Right: Our carpet bedding design illustrated a butterfly, which was a popular Victorian motif in gardens.

Below: Vegetable gardens were no longer hidden from view, and kitchen gardens became a status symbol and design feature in their own right.

Carpet bedding still had a place in this later Victorian garden and proved to be an excellent vehicle for using the popular new dwarf plants with their eye-catching foliage. In our garden the bedding design was copied from an 1875 plan of a butterfly, and then constructed using the contemporary method of a card template and sand.

In this period, too, fruit and vegetables for the first time became fashionable plants not just to be cultivated but, for the first time, to be seen. The pressure on gardeners to grow a variety of vegetables all year round lead to some experimentation with techniques to achieve this.

At RHS Harlow Carr we reconstructed one such invention – the hotbed. It was a simple enough construction, but it made all the difference in bringing crops on early. Our hotbed was made by placing a wooden frame on the ground and then filling it with 6 inches of quality top soil, which was then planted up and covered with a glass top. Here we planted Victorian Long Green Ridge cucumber. The rest of our vegetable garden played host to other contemporary favourites such as sweet peas, purple podded and rubins egg beans, parsley, ruby chard, bull's blood beetroot, Golden Ball turnips, Russian red kale, blackcurrants and gooseberries.

PLANT LIST

Acer palmatum 'Ôsakazuki'
Acer palmatum 'Atropurpureum'
Acer japonicum 'Aconitifolium'
Acer shirasawanum 'Aureum'
Acer palmatum
Rhododendron 'Gloria Mundi'
Rhododendron 'Sang de Gentbrugge'
Rhododendron 'Pallas'
Viburnum plicatum
Hydrangea aspera subsp. *sargentiana*
Syringa vulgaris 'Andenken an Ludwig Späth'
Enkianthus campanulatus
Hebe odora
Hebe 'Autumn Glory'
Vinca minor
Pleioblastus viridistriatus
Shibataea kumasaca
Phyllostachys aurea
Fargesia nitida
Semiarundinaria fastuosa
Lespedeza thunbergii
Rhododendron 'Amoenena'
Rhododendron 'Daviesii'
Festuca glauca
Hydrangea macrophylla 'Nigra'
Vinca major 'Variegata'
Pachysandra terminalis
Epimedium x *perralchicum* 'Frohnleiten'

Aquilegia vulgaris
Filipendula vulgaris 'Multiplex'
Diervilla x *splendens*
Euonymus alatus
Tellima grandiflora
Francoa sonchifolia
Rhododendron 'Pink Pearl'
Rhododendron 'John Waterer'
Geranium phaeum 'Samobor'
Shibataea kumasaca

Matterhorn

Pinus sylvestris
Pinus mugo Pumilo Group
Pinus sylvestris 'Watererii'
Pinus mugo

Trees

Liquidambar styraciflua
Catalpa bignonioides
Magnolia x *soulangeana*
Cercidiphyllum japonicum
Prunus pendula 'Pendula Rubra'
Apple 'Brownlees Russet'
Apple 'Irish Peach'
Apple 'Lady Henniker'
Apple 'Golden Spire'
Apple 'Allington Pippin'
Apple 'Peasgood's Nonsuch'
Apple 'Bramley's Seedling'
Apple 'Cox's Orange Pippin'

Rosa 'Louise Odier'
Rosa 'Tuscany Superb'

Edwardian Garden 1901–30
RHS Garden Harlow Carr, Yorkshire

1 Slate roof on
   summerhouse
2 Sunken pool
3 Rill
4 Urn
5 Rose garden
6 Topiary
7 Seat
   (reconstituted stone)
8 Wild garden
9 Wooden bench
10 Large terracotta pot
11 Mown path

Women were playing a part in garden design at the start of the twentieth century, and this garden echoes the distinctive style of one of the most prominent female designers of the time, Gertrude Jekyll.

Jekyll's designs could work in any size garden and her key element was her use of colour, which she used to great effect in her signature feature – the herbaceous border. The revival of the herbaceous border was a reaction against the earlier, garish, Italianate bedding schemes and Jekyll's approach was much more subtle with plants laid out in drifts graduating from hot to really cool colours.

Working alongside architect Edwin Lutyens, Jekyll transformed the look of British gardens; her colourful, informal planting was the perfect accompaniment to his formal hard landscaping. To enter our garden at RHS Harlow Carr you must pass through a Lutyens trademark – a summerhouse laid with a floor of intricately up-ended tiles. Beyond this is another Lutyens' trademark – a sunken pool fed with water falling from a stone rill and surrounded by wide stone paths, walls and flower borders. The pond itself provided the perfect showcase for one of the latest plant fashions – the water lily. At RHS Harlow Carr we planted the popular *Nymphaea gladstonia*. Contemporary style gurus recommended the sparing use of garden ornamentation, so this garden was dressed simply with an urn above the rill and another in a corner of the garden to act as focal points.

Thanks to the explorations of the plant hunters in the Victorian age, a wider variety of plants were being used, including many new exotics. In this garden we used sorbus from China, amallanchia from North America and magnolia from Japan, but lest we forget that we are in an English garden, beyond the exotics we planted a meadow of more familiar plants, such as cornflowers and poppies.

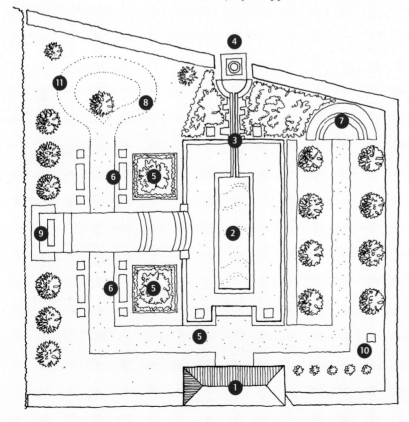

PLANT LIST

Rosa 'Madame Plantier'
Rosmarinus officinalis
Perovskia atriplicifolia 'Blue
  Spire'
Sorbaria tomentosa
Rosa 'Céleste'
Pyrus salicifolia
Olearia phlogopappa
Yucca filamentosa
  'Variegata'
Perovskia atriplicifolia 'Blue
  Spire'
Cistus 'Grayswood Pink'
Ceanothus 'Gloire de
  Versailles'
Rosa 'Maiden's Blush'
Philadelphus 'Virginal'
Buddleja alternifolia
Syringa vulgaris 'Madame
  Lemoine'
Cotinus coggygria
Nepeta x faassenii
Anemone hupehensis var.
  japonica
Saponaria officinalis
  'Double Form'
Eryngium 'Miss Willmott's
  Ghost'
Stachys byzantina
Penstemon 'Evelyn'

Shrubs for wild garden
Rosa moyesii
Viburnum opulus
Euonymus europaeus
Corylopsis pauciflora
Elaeagnus 'Quicksilver'

Amelanchier canadensis
Buddleja var. nanhoensis
Prunus padus
Crataegus persimilis
  'Prunifolia Splendens'

Plants for summerhouse
Rosa 'Goldfinch'
Clematis montana
Rosa 'Paul's Scarlet
  Climber'
Vitis vinifera 'Purpurea'
Clematis cirrhosa
Rosa 'Paul Transon'
Campsis radicans

Trees
Corylus avellana
Malus 'John Downie'
Malus floribunda
Malus x purpurea
Davidia involucrata
Mespilus germanica
Sorbus hupehensis
Prunus cerasifera
Magnolia stellata

Herbaceous border
Aster x frikartii 'Mönch'
Campanula 'Kent Belle'
Anchusa 'Loddon Royalist'
Delphinium 'Harlequin'
Clematis recta
Tradescantia virginiana
Ceratostigma
  willmottianum
Achillea 'The Pearl'
Gypsophila paniculata

Filipendula camtschatica
Helianthus 'Lemon Queen'
Verbascum chaixii
Coreopsis verticillata
Artemesia stelleriana
Helenium 'Moerheim
  Beauty'
Macleaya cordata
Geum 'Mrs J. Bradshaw'
Euphorbia griffithii
Inula magnifica
Papaver orientale
Lychnis chalcedonica
Potentilla 'Gibson's Scarlet'
Monarda didyma
  'Cambridge Red'
Crocosmia x crocosmiiflora
Rudbeckia laciniata
  'Hortensia'
Helianthus 'Loddon Gold'
Achillea 'Gold Plate'
Helenium autumnale
Papaver rupifragum
Meconopsis cambrica
Hemerocallis fulva 'Flore
  Pleno'
Kniphofia 'Bees' Lemon'
Thalictrum flavum
Actaea simplex 'Prichard's
  Giant'
Cephalaria gigantea
Artemisia stelleriana
Penstemon heterophyllus
Limonium platyphyllum
Phlox paniculata 'Amethyst'
Eupatorium purpureum
Echinops ritro
Crambe cordifolia

Thalictrum aquilegiifolium
Campanula glomerata
Campanula pyramidalis
Iris pallida subsp. pallida
Phlomis fruticosa
Clematis montana
Rosa 'Goldfinch'
Vitis vinifera 'Purpurea'
Clematis cirrhosa
Campsis radicans

Rose beds and
sunken plants
Rosa 'Goldfinch'
Rosa 'Paul's Scarlet
  Climber'
Rosa 'Paul Transon'
Rosa 'Madame Caroline
  Testout'
Rosa 'Killarney'
Rosa 'Old Blush China'
Rosa 'Madame Abel
  Chatenay'
Bergenia cordifolia
Nepeta x faassenii
Paeonia 'Sarah Bernhardt'
Lilium regale
Delphinium 'Piccolo'
Centranthus ruber
Paeonia 'Duchesse de
  Nemours'
Dianthus plumarius
Aubrieta deltoidea
Ceratostigma
  plumbaginoides
Campanula
  portenschlagiana
Artemisia arborescens

Lithodora diffusa
Iberis sempervirens
Cistus x dansereaui
  'Decumbens'
Cerastium tomentosum
Parahebe lyallii
Hyssopus officinalis
Lavandula angustifolia
  'Munstead'
Anemone hupehensis var.
  japonica
Iris pallida subsp. pallida
Dryas octopetala

Above and top:
The Edwardian garden at
RHS Harlow Carr carefully
recreated the balanced
landscaping and planting
for which Jekyll and Lutyens
are best known.

Festival of Britain Garden 1930–59
RHS Garden Harlow Carr, Yorkshire

The 1950s saw a postwar style boom and the emergence of a look that was modern and cutting edge. In the garden this often meant the landscaping was dominated by concrete – which was the designers' choice as well as being a cheap and widely available material. The new garden was influenced by the art and architecture of the time and bore no resemblance to any garden style that had preceded it. Our garden was very much influenced by one of the trendsetters of the day, Christopher Tunnard, whose gardens were designed to complement concrete modern houses.

Practicality was integral to the modern style and often manifested itself as places for rest and recreation; plants were used to add to the design, provide texture and soften the effect of the hard concrete. Simplicity was fundamental to the modern look, as was a lack of decoration or fussy borders.

Our garden echoes these rules of design and is simply laid out so as not to detract from the view through a frame at the end. This was a modernist conceit that echoed earlier ideas of 'borrowing' landscape and served to link the garden and the world beyond in order to give the garden a sense of place. These 'picture frames' were usually made of wood or concrete – in our garden we used wood. These vertical accents were

1 Maria Shepherd pots
2 L-shaped flowerbed
3 Steps
4 *Rhus glabra laciniata*
5 Dawyck beech
6 Rose beds
7 Hepworth sculpture
8 Wooden screen

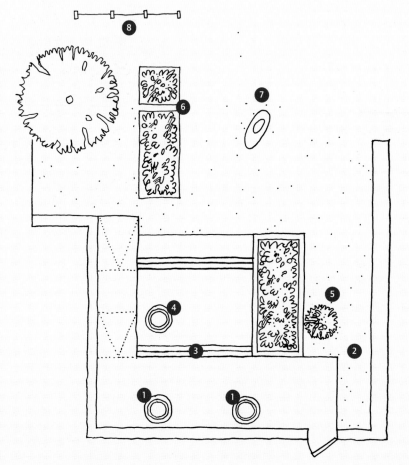

included to counteract the horizontal lines of these gardens, and could also be provided by plants – we used a dawyck beech to draw the eye upwards and to create volume and form within the garden. Of course, for designers of these modern gardens the purpose of the tree was to create a sculptural effect rather than to be appreciated for its horticultural merit.

To soften our concrete paving, we planted an L-shaped bed and mass-planted foliage plants that will grow and spread and will help to break up the hard landscaping. Planting schemes in these 50s'-style gardens also featured as massed beds of flowers of a single colour, and at RHS Harlow Carr we echoed this fashion by planting a raised concrete bed with bright marigolds. Roses were another favourite for this style, and the most popular rose of the period was the hybrid tea. In two beds beyond the patio we planted blocks of one of the most popular post-war roses, *Rosa* 'Peace'. Rhus, or smooth summer, is a dramatic architectural plant; its striking foliage turns gold and red in the autumn, which serves to brighten up the concrete patio throughout the year.

PLANT LIST

Hamamelis x *intermedia* 'Jelena'
Rubus cockburnianus
Lonicera pileata
Hebe rakaiensis
Genista hispanica
Rubus tricolor
Cytisus x *praecox* 'Albus'
Hebe pinguifolia 'Pagei'
Rosa 'Peace'
Rhus glabra 'Laciniata'

Above: Golden marigolds add a dramatic splash of colour and a soft texture to the otherwise cold concrete terracing of our post-war garden at RHS Harlow Carr.

Outdoor Room 1960–80
RHS Garden Harlow Carr, Yorkshire

1 Pergola
2 Paving
3 Sunken pool
4 Architectural plants
   in gravel
5 Brick paving
6 Stepping stones/
   ground cover planting

Gardens in the 1970s were all about creating an outdoor room and a low-maintenance space for the whole family to enjoy. With this format John Brookes revolutionized garden design in late twentieth century and made a huge impact on suburban gardens. The greatest appeal of this look was that it was simple to achieve.

John Brookes' trademark feature was his use of hard materials, particularly gravel, around planting so as to cover every inch of bare soil and restrict any growth of weeds. Another method of keeping down weeds and thus ensuring a low-maintenance garden encouraged a new planting craze – ground cover planting. In the past this had manifested itself as a lawn, but now there was no time to mow a lawn, so another material was needed to cover larger areas in gardens. Ground cover was created using low-growing plants that tended to grow quickly by trailing and clumping to create an informal,

carpet effect. We used the most popular plant of the time in our garden, the *Juniper squamata* 'Blue Carpet'. We also planted a drift of sarcocca at the base of the birch trees to run into the junipers to contrast leaf shape and colour.

Patios and paving played an important part in the outdoor room, providing a place for entertaining, eating and on which children could play. The Outdoor Room garden at RHS Harlow Carr included such paved areas, but also included a surface made from bricks laid on end. These were set by brushing gravel in the gaps between them in which plants can self seed and soften the landscaping. We also included stepping stones through gravel.

But planting style was not just restricted to ground cover: architectural plants also featured in this period style. In these low-maintenance gardens these plants served to

break up the hard surfaces, and big, bold plants were carefully placed for maximum effect.

We planted *Fatsia japonica* for its size, glossy texture and evergreen nature, along with spiky phormiums as dramatic punctuation. Plants also served to soften another popular 1970s' garden structure – the pergola. People had seen pergolas on Mediterranean holidays and wanted one back at home to re-create *al fresco* living. In the Harlow Carr garden we used a pergola to blur the line between the house and garden and to visually and physically lead you outside. The traditional style of planting rambling roses over these constructions had been dismissed, however, and the new fashion was for growing vines and honeysuckles to re-create the authentic Mediterranean dining experience. At RHS Harlow Carr we planted *Lonicera japonica* 'Halliana', a honeysuckle.

Influenced by these Mediterranean holidays, plants such as figs and herbs featured strongly in gardens as decorative rather than functional plants. In our herb corner, we planted rosemary, mint, sage and thyme around a dramatic centrepiece of fennel.

PLANT LIST

Cordyline australis
Fatsia japonica
Paeonia delavayi var. *lutea*
Phormium tenax
Cotoneaster horizontalis
Aralia elata
Gleditsia triacanthos
Helleborus argutifolius
Mahonia x *media* 'Charity'
Phormium tenax
   Purpureum Group
Rosa glauca
Euphorbia characias subsp.
   wulfenii
Viburnum plicatum f.
   tomentosum 'Mariesii'
Salvia officinalis
   'Purpurascens'
Tiarella cordifolia 'Iron
   Butterfly'
Juniperus squamata 'Blue
   Carpet'
Sarcococca confusa
Viburnum davidii
Pulmonaria 'Sissinghurst
   White'
Cornus sericea 'Flaviramea'
Salix alba subsp. *vitellina*
   'Britzensis'
Juniperus x *pfitzeriana*
   'Kuriwao Gold'
Ficus carica
Rheum palmatum
   'Atrosanguineum'
Juniperus sabina
   'Tamariscifolia'
Phyllostachys nigra

Herbs

Salvia officinalis
Chives
Mint
Thymus vulgaris
Rosmarinus officinalis
   'Benenden Blue'
Fennel

Herbaceous

Alchemilla mollis
Acanthus mollis
Acanthus spinosus
Verbascum bombyciferum
Kniphofia caulescens
Cosmos atrosanguineus
Onopordum acanthium
Crocosmia 'Lucifer'

Pergola

Lonicera japonica 'Halliana'
Clematis montana

Bank

Juniperus x *pfitzeriana*
   'Wilhelm Pfitzer'
Cotoneaster dammeri
Rosa 'Lady Penzance'
Juniperus sabina
   'Tamariscifolia'

Above and top: The Outdoor Room of the 60s and 70s was very much influenced by holidaymakers keen to re-create their Mediterranean evenings back at home. Water features and pergolas were an essential element of the look.

Twenty-first Century Garden 2004
RHS Garden Harlow Carr, Yorkshire

The final garden at RHS Harlow Carr brings our story of 200 years of garden design right up to date. Although developed for a modern, design-conscious family in an urban space, this garden also echoes many of the ideas and styles of the other historical reconstructions. But of all the garden styles represented at RHS Harlow Carr, this is closest in vision to the Edwardian garden, where hard landscaping and planting are balanced and working together.

Located at the edge of the site at Harlow Carr, the plot is flanked by a busy road, so some hard landscaping was needed to diffuse the noise of the traffic. Within the boundary walls another oval wall was built, using a combination of hard-wearing steel and western red cedar which added a cutting-edge, but luxurious, touch. The garden room was constructed from steel and glass and provides the ultimate 'room outside' for use in all weathers.

Another design feature that is finding its place in modern gardens is lighting. Formerly used primarily for security or safety, experiments with lighting have led to it being used as a feature in its own right. In this garden coloured lights and fibre optics highlight features in the garden or provide glittering stars in a starless night sky. Reflecting the view that the twenty-first century urban garden is not just an oasis for relaxation but is also a place to entertain and be entertained, this garden is also equipped with a DVD player and projector for outdoor film viewing.

1 Wall set with fibre optics
2 Birch trees
3 Steel and glass garden room
4 *Catalpa bignonioides* (Indian bean tree)
5 *Dicksonia antarcticas*
6 Lawn
7 Steel and western red cedar wall
8 *Trachycarpus fortunei*
9 Natural local stone patio

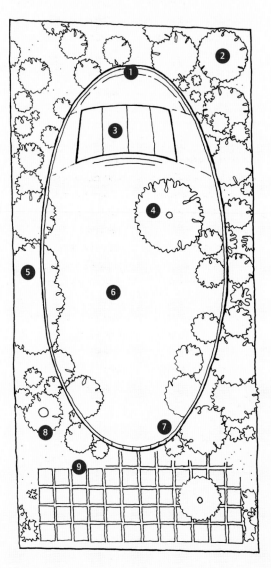

PLANT LIST

Rosmarinus officinalis
Alchemilla mollis
Phormium 'Sunset'
Rosa Mortimer Sackler
Trachycarpus fortunei
Polystichum polyblepharum
Rhododendron 'Vulcan'
Pyrus communis 'Doyenne du Comice'
Viburnum plicatum f. *tomentosum* 'Lanarth'
Rosa Snow Goose
Lonicera japonica 'Hall's Prolific'
Sarcococca confusa
Hedera helix 'Butterfingers'
Liriope muscari 'Variegata'
Betula nigra 'Heritage'
Viburnum tinus 'French White'
Passiflora caerulea
Hydrangea arborescens 'Annabelle'
Nepeta 'Six Hills Giant'
Verbascum olympicum
Hemerocallis 'Corky'
Ceanothus 'Blue Mound'
Solanum crispum 'Glasnevin'
Dicksonia antarctica
Buddleja davidii 'Black Knight'
Sedum 'Herbstfreude'
Catalpa bignonioides 'Aurea'
Salvia officinalis

Echinops ritro
Rudbeckia fulgida var. *sullivantii* 'Goldsturm'
Kniphofia 'Nancy's Red'
Ligularia przewalskii
Humulus lupulus 'Aureus'
Crocosmia x *crocosmiiflora* 'Star of the East'
Callicarpa bodinieri var. *giraldii* 'Profusion'
Skimmia japonica 'Rubella'
Hypericum x *inodorum*
Garrya elliptica 'James Roof'
Fatsia japonica
Lonicera henryi
Crataegus viridis 'Winter King'
Aucuba japonica
Vinca minor 'Aureovariegata'
Vinca minor 'Atropurpurea'
Polypodium vulgare
Thymus vulgaris
Rosa 'Parkdirektor Riggers'
Rosa 'Compassion'
Parsley
Mint
Sorbus 'Sunshine'

A mix of formal and informal planting styles echoes the informal area outside the oval structure and its more formal design inside. Outside the oval walls the planting is almost wild and made up of hardy plants – both natives and exotics. To create immediate impact, mature specimens of trees were used – birch, *Dicksonia antarctica*, *Trachycarpus fortunei* – which were then underplanted with ferns.

Inside the oval walls the style is more controlled, with a neat lawn punctuated by an Indian bean tree, a structural piece that links all the elements of the garden together.

Selected gardens to visit

Some gardens do not have telephone numbers (they are private or run by charities). Alton Towers has one but only for the theme park.

Chapter 1

ALTON TOWERS
Alton, Stoke-on-Trent, Staffordshire ST10 4DB
www.altontowers.com

ROYAL BOTANIC GARDENS
Kew, Richmond, Surrey TW9 3AB
T 020 8940 1171
www.kew.org

ALVERSTOKE CRESCENT GARDENS
Gosport, Hampshire PO12 2DP
This twentieth-century recreation of an early nineteenth-century garden is open all day, every day

DERBY ARBORETUM
Arboretum Square, Derby DE23 8FN
Open all day, every day

SCOTNEY CASTLE
Lamberhurst, Tunbridge Wells, Kent TN3 8JN
T 01892 891081
www.nationaltrust.org.uk

GUNNERSBURY PARK AND MUSEUM
Popes Lane, Acton, London W3 8LQ
T 020 8992 1612

Chapter 2

UNIVERSITY BOTANIC GARDEN
Cambridge CB2 1JF
T 01223 336265

TRENTHAM GARDENS
Stone Road, Stoke-on-Trent, Staffordshire ST4 8AX
T 01782 657341

BIDDULPH GRANGE
Stoke-on-Trent, Staffordshire ST8 7SD
T 01782 517999
www.nationaltrust.org.uk

CHATSWORTH
Bakewell, Derbyshire DE45 1PP
T 01246 582204

SHRUBLAND PARK
Coddenham, Ipswich, Suffolk IP6 9OP
T 01473 830221

WADDESDON MANOR
Waddesdon, Aylesbury, Buckinghamshire HP18 0JH
T 01296 653211
www.waddesdon.org.uk

Chapter 3

BATTERSEA PARK
Albert Bridge Road, London SW11 4NJ
T 020 8871 8800

ELVASTON CASTLE
Borrowash Road, Elvaston, Derbyshire DE72 3EP
T 01332 571342

RENISHAW
Renishaw, Sheffield, South Yorkshire S31 9WB
www.sitwell.co.uk

BODNANT
Tel-Y-Cafn, Colwyn Bay, Wales LL28 5RE
T 01492 650460
www.nationaltrust.org.uk

GRAVETYE MANOR
(now a hotel)
East Grinstead, West Sussex RH19 4LI
T 01342 810567

CAERHAYS CASTLE
Caerhays, Gorran, St Austell, Cornwall PL26 6LY
T 01872 501310
www.caerhays.co.uk

Chapter 4

THE GARDENS OF EASTON LODGE
Great Dunmow, Essex CM6 2BB
T 01371 876979

THE ROOF GARDEN
99 Kensington High Street, London W8 5ED
T 020 7937 7994

RHS GARDEN WISLEY
Woking, Surrey GU23 6QB
T 01483 224234
www.rhs.org.uk

HESTERCOMBE
Chedden Fitzpaine, Taunton, Somerset TA8 LQ
T 01823 413923

TINTINHULL HOUSE
Tintinhull, Yeovil, Somerset BA22 8PZ
T 01935 8225545
www.nationaltrust.org.uk

SISSINGHURST CASTLE
Sissinghurst, Cranbrook, Kent TN17 2AB
T 01580 715330

HIDCOTE
Hidcote Bartrim, Chipping Camden, Gloucestershire GL55 6LR
T 01386 438333

THE GIBBERD GARDEN
Marsh Lane, Gilden Way, Harlow, Essex CM17 0NA
T 01279 442112

GREAT DIXTER
Dixter Road, Northiam, Kent TN31 6PH
T 01797 252878
www.greatdixter.co.uk

Chapter 5

DARTINGTON HALL
Dartington, Totnes, Devon TQ9 6EL
T 01803 862367

ST CATHERINE'S COLLEGE
Oxford OX1 3UJ
T 01865 271702
By appointment only

JELLICOE'S 'SKY GARDEN'
on the roof of House of Fraser in Guildford
01483 307400
or Albert Roux Café
01483 301661

THE SIR HAROLD HILLIER GARDEN AND ARBORETUM
Jermyn's Lane, Ampfield, Romsey, Hampshire SO51 0QA
T 01794 368787

THE SAVILL GARDEN
Windsor Great Park,
Wick Lane,
Englefield Green TW20 0UU
T 01753 847518

LITTLE PEACOCKS
(Colvin and Moggridge
Landscape)
Filkins, Oxfordshire.
Opens through the
National Gardens Scheme
www.ngs.org.uk

BETH CHATTO GARDENS
Elmstead Market,
Colchester CO7 7DB
T 01206 822007
www.bethchatto.co.uk

Chapter 6
WESTBURY COURT
Westbury-on-Severn,
Gloucestershire GL14 1PD
T 01452 760461
www.nationaltrust.org.uk

SHUTE HOUSE
Donhead St Mary,
Shaftesbury,
Dorset SP7 9DG
T 01747 828866
By appointment only

SUTTON PLACE
Guildford, Surrey GU4 7QV
T 01483 504455.
As I write, the estate is on
the market, so visitors must
ring to check the position

DENMANS
Fontwell, Arundel,
West Sussex BN18 0SU
T 01243 542808

RHS GARDEN ROSEMOOR
Great Torrington,
Devon EX38 8PH
T 01805 624067
www.rhs.org.uk

RHS GARDEN HYDE HALL
Rettendon, Chelmsford,
Essex CM3 8ET
T 01245 400256
www.rhs.org.uk

RHS GARDEN HARLOW CARR
Beckwithshaw, Harrogate,
North Yorks HG3 1QB
T 01423 565418
www.rhs.org.uk

RYTON ORGANIC GARDENS
Ryton-on-Dunsmore,
Coventry,
Warwickshire CV8 3LG
T 024 7630 3517

THE MUSEUM OF GARDEN
HISTORY
Lambeth Palace Road,
London SE1 7LB
T 020 7401 8865
www.museumgardenhistory.
org

Chapter 7
EDEN PROJECT
Bodelva, St Austell,
Cornwall PL24 2SG
T 01726 81191
www.edenproject.com

NATIONAL BOTANIC GARDEN
OF WALES
Middleton Hall, Llanarthne,
Camarthenshire SA32 8HB
T 01558 667132

GROOMBRIDGE PLACE
Tunbridge Wells,
Kent TN3 9QG
T 01892 863999

TREVANO ESTATE AND
GARDENS AND THE NATIONAL
MUSEUM OF GARDENING
Helston,
Cornwall TR13 0RU
T 01326 574274

ANTONY
Torpoint,
Cornwall PL11 2QA
T 01752 812364

WESTONBIRT FESTIVAL OF
GARDENS
information site
www.festivalofgardens.co.uk

CHAUMONT-SUR-LOIRE
INTERNATIONAL GARDEN
FESTIVAL
Ferme du Chateau, 41150,
Chaumont-sur-Loire, France

ALNWICK CASTLE
Alnwick,
Northumberland NE66 1NQ
T 01665 511350
www.alnwickgarden.com

Royal Horticultural
Society
www.rhs.org.uk
T 020 7828 4125
(Vincent Square)

National Gardens Scheme
www.ngs.org.uk
T 01483 211535

Index

Picture credits

BBC Worldwide wishes to thank the following for providing photographs and for permission to reproduce copyright material. While every effort has been made to trace and acknowledge copyright holders, we would like to apologize should there be any errors or omissions.

All photographs by Robin Matthews © BBC Worldwide Ltd except:

The Advertising Archive Ltd 35, 175;
Arcaid 92 (© Richard Bryant), 126–7 (© Alan Weintraub);
The Art Archive 67b, 79;
Battersea Park 76, 77 (by courtesy Patrick Leuby); 136, 137;
BBC Photo Library 118–19, 120, 139, 160, 177t, 178;
BBC Gardeners World Magazine 177b (Susan Bell), 188 (George Brooks);
Bloom Pictures/© Richard Bloom 155;
Bridgeman Art Library 15 (City of Westminster Archive Centre, London, UK), 18–19, 46–7, 48 (The Stapleton Collection), 30–1 (Ipswich Borough Council Museums & Galleries, Suffolk, UK);
Jonathan Buckley 12;
George Carter 173;
Clapham Church, Lancashire 82;
Concrete Information Ltd/ Mrs Sheila Harrison, sculptor: William Mitchell 124;

Cooper & Taylor, Landscape Design Ltd 186–7;
Corbis/© Michael Boys 151, 152;
Country Life Picture Library 78, 81, 89, 101, 121, 130, 131; 125 (Vivian Russell);
Edifice 88 (Philippa Lewis), 122 (Lewis-Darley);
Mary Evans Picture Library 14tr, 36, 40, 46, 60, 65, 67t, 111;
Garden Exposures Photo Library/© Andrea Jones 190–1;
Garden & Wildlife Matters 55; 174 © Jeremy Hoare; 176;
Garden Photo Library/© Derek St Romaine 192;
Garden Picture Library 68bl, 70;
GardenWorld Images 43 (I Anderson), 172; 198 (T McGlinchey);
© John Glover 49, 73, 84, 154t;
Gravetye Manor Hotel & Restaurant/Hugh Palmer 69;
Harpur Garden Library 26, 41, 44–5, 66, 71, 74–5, 95, 96–7, 129, 163, 179, 184, 193 © Jerry Harpur; 98, 147 © Marcus Harpur;
© Hulton|Archive/Getty Images 59 (Terry Fincher); 62–3, 80; 103 (Lisa Sheridan); 104–5, 113; 140–1 (George W Hales); 161;
Charles Jencks 182;
courtesy Kensington Roof Gardens 109;
Rose Keyes 7;
Andew Lawson 24, 33, 107, 154b, 171, 180–1, 195, 201;
Andrew Lawson/HRH Prince of Wales 162;
Lockbund Sculpture/Andrew Lawson 185;

Marianne Majerus 183, 194;
Museum of Garden History 14b, 16, 20 b, 90, 91, 93 t & b, 94, 104, 114, 116, 123 t & b, 124l, 145, 149 t & b, 150l;
The National Archives Image Library 57, 85, 112;
By courtesy of the National Portrait Gallery, London 37; 68tl (Bassano);
National Trust Photographic Library 148 (Andrew Lawson); 51, 52–3 (Nick Meers); 21, 164 (Stephen Robson); 6, 39 (Ian Shaw); 22–3 (Andy Williams); 167 (Mike Williams);
Clive Nichols 143, 156–7, 158–9, 168–9;
By courtesy Notcutts Ltd 150r;
Graeme Peacock 196;
Royal Botanic Gardens, Kew 1, 50;
Royal Horticultural Society, Lindley Library 8–9 (background), 13, 14tl, 29, 38, 58 (background), 68br, 83, 76–7 (background), 86, 100, 108;
TopFoto 87 (British Library/HIP), 42 (Corporation of London/HIP), 64, 134 (National Archives/HIP), 110 (Topham);
© Jo Whitworth 132, 135, 154c;
© Rob Whitworth 133.

Acknowledgements

Thanks to garden creators and commentators, alive and dead, who make garden history such a rich subject. Some in particular have shared their garden passions with me and educated me: Gaie Houston; Toby Owen; Mavis Batey; Dominic Cole; Guy Cooper; John Brookes; Brent Elliott; Ivan Hicks; Charles Jencks; Peter Smithers; Gordon Taylor; Rosemary Verey; and all my friends at the Oxfordshire Gardens Trust.

As far as this book is concerned I would like to give particular thanks to Mavis Batey; John Brookes; Guy Cooper; Brent Elliott; Toby Owen; and Gordon Taylor who read and criticised my manuscript; to my children Rose and Miranda whose good company and PA skills keep me on track; and to Mark Lucas who is to literary agency what David Beckham is to football.

Many others have helped, advised, guided and encouraged me, and I am grateful to them all: Gaynor Aalternon; Pat Adams; Paula Al-Lach; Jennie Allen; James Alexander-Sinclair; David Barnes; Andrew Barron; Helena Bellhouse; Alison Benton; Stephen Bennett; Marcia and Michael Blakenham; Viv Bowler; Christopher Bradley-Hole; George Brock; Helena Caldon; John Clowes; Hester Cohen; Andrew Colquhoun; Vicky Darby; Les Davis; Mark Fane; Katie Fretwell; Owen Gay; Elizabeth Gilbert; Bethan Greenhaulgh; Francesca Greenoak; Ian Hamilton Finlay; Chris Harnet; Dianne Harris; University of Illinois; Jay Hunt; Sheila Harvey; Felicity Hawkins; Michael Heseltine; Sue Hopper; Gaie Houston; Winsome Houston; Becky Jones-Owen; Rachel Jordan; Peter King; Robin Lane Fox; Susanne Mitchell; Hal Moggridge; Roddy Llewellyn; Jennie Lowe; Gemma Martin; George C. McGavin; Charles Mills; William Notcutt; Juliette Otterburn Hall; Jo Owen; Lynn Palmer; Nic Patten; Will Pearson; Kate Pickard; David Pogson; Gareth Pottle; Peter Powell; Susan and David Jackson; Pam John; Tony Johnson; Alice Saunders; Peter Smithers; Joel Richards; Viv Robinson; Jane Root; Hiroko Saito; Lakhan Samuels; Mark Stephens; Bill Stokes; Hiromi Takahashi; Celia Taylor; Simon Thornton Wood; Edgar Vincent; Charles Wace; Marion Warden; Sarah Warwick; Donald Waterer; Louise Wellesley; Kim Wilde; Tom Wright; Hannah Wyatt.

BBC2; BBC Worldwide; Buckingham Palace; Carterton Library; Cement and Concrete Association; Council of Mortgage Lenders; The Garden History Society; GreenSpace; Hatchards; The Henry Doubleday Research Association; the Horticultural Trades Association; Institute of Landscape Architects; Kernock Park Plants; the Lindley Library; The National Trust; Office for National Statistics; Oxford University Museum of Natural History; The National Gardens Scheme; the Royal Botanic Gardens; Kew; the Royal Horticultural Society; Royal Horticultural Society Japan; Scotts; The Times; Trades Union Congress library; Two Four television; V&A national art library and the print room; Westminster public libraries.

Finally my heartfelt thanks to the owners of all the gardens – big, minute and in between – that I have visited over the last 20 years.

Jane Owen 2004